Who Am I?

What the Bible teaches about Christian Identity

by

Terry Johnson

EP BOOKS (Evangelical Press)

Registered Office: 140 Coniscliffe Road, Darlington, Co. Durham, UK DL3 7RT

www.epbooks.org
admin@epbooks.org

EP Books are distributed in the USA by:

JPL Books
www.jplbooks.com
orders@jplbooks.com

and

1oofThose Ltd
www.1oofthose.com
sales.us@1oofthose.com

First published 2020

British Library Cataloguing in Publication Data available

ISBN 978-1-78397-277-7

Table of Contents

I. Opening Considerations

1. Salvation and Identity

And we know that for those who love God all things work together for good, for those who are called according to his purpose. For those whom he foreknew he also predestined to be conformed to the image of his Son, in order that he might be the firstborn among many brothers. And those whom he predestined he also called, and those whom he called he also justified, and those whom he justified he also glorified. (Romans 8:28–30)

When I was a boy my mother bought us children a "Mr. Potato Head" kit. It consisted of a variety of noses, eyes, ears, lips, arms, hands, legs, feet, and so on. Add a potato from the pantry, stick-in the various appendages, and presto, a hilarious looking Mr. Potato Head; hilarious because everything was out of proportion: massive body, little tooth-pick legs and arms, huge ears, bulbous nose, big lips, and giant eyes. Everything was comically out of balance. Remove Potato Head's smile and replace it with a frowning visage, and he becomes a monster.

Theological balances

We begin our consideration of identity with a discussion of balance. The above passage, with its "golden chain" of salvation, as it has been known in the Reformed church, presents each item of the *ordo salutus*, the "order of salvation," as a link in an unbroken chain. It begins with election/predestination, moves along to justification (faith and repentance unstated but implied given what preceded in Romans 3–5), adoption, sanctification ("conformed to the image of His Son"), glorification, and since glorification, perseverance. At any given moment Scripture may speak of our whole salvation as one of these items, or as the *ordo* as a completed whole. We are those "chosen by God" (1 Peter 2:4), "justified by faith" (Romans 5:1), "adopt(ed) as sons" (Ephesians 1:5), "sanctified by the Spirit" (Romans 15:16), who will endure to the end (Matthew 24:13). We are saved (Ephesians 2:8) and are being saved (1 Corinthians 1:18).

The Bible is richly diverse in the ways that it presents salvation. Multiple metaphors addressing multiple human needs calling for various saving responses are employed. Each of these metaphors is a window through which we are able to gain a glimpse of sin (the fundamental need), the cross (the fundamental solution), and faith (the fundamental response).

For example, Jesus says, "I am the Bread of Life" (John 6:35). Here sin is represented by the yearnings of the soul; Jesus presents Himself as the One who can satisfy our spiritual hunger and quench our spiritual thirst, eating and drinking illustrating coming to Jesus and believing in Him.

Jesus also says "I am the light of the world" (John 8:12). Darkness represents the ignorance and moral evil of sin. Jesus presents Himself as the One who dispels that ignorance and evil; salvation means following Jesus by walking in His light. Jesus says, "I am the True Vine" (John 15:1). Salvation is represented as branches remaining connected ("abiding") to the Vine through which they are able to have life and to bear fruit. Salvation can be represented as rebirth (John 3:1ff), as justification (Romans 5:1), as redemption (Romans 3:24; Ephesians 1:7), as propitiation (Romans 3:25; 1 John 2:2), as reconciliation with God (Romans 5:10; 2 Corinthians 5:18–21), as adoption (Romans 8:15; Galatians 4:4–5; Ephesians 1:5), as sanctification (Romans 8:29; Ephesians 1:4), as perseverance (Romans 5:3; Matthew 24:13), and as the event by which salvation is completed, glorification (Romans 8:30). Scripture may employ the language of blood sacrifice, of the law-court, of relationships, of the marketplace, of the battlefield, of athletic competition, and of family relations to make the point. Salvation can be identified as one item in the *ordo salutus*, or as the whole *ordo*.

Imbalances

However, the gospel gets warped when we allow one item to become the exclusive metaphor by which our gospel is defined. So does our self-awareness, our self-concept, our identity. The result: Christian Potato Heads. Repeatedly this has happened in the history of the church. Never has the outcome been good. Here is a standard *ordo*, understanding each item as realized in union with Christ, by whom we are justified, sanctified, glorified, and all the rest.

- Election
- Effectual call (regeneration)
- Faith & Repentance
- Justification
- Adoption
- Sanctification

- Perseverance

- Glorification

At one time or another each of these items has become the whole gospel for a group or a movement. Disproportion inevitably has created a comic counterfeit of the gospel. Yet distorted spiritual truths can never be considered funny. Imbalance ultimately creates a spiritual monster, a frowning and destructive Potato Head, and a warped and harmful identity.

Election

Let's start at the top. What happens when we make the whole gospel equal to election? "You did not choose me but I chose you," John told the disciples (John 15:16). Election is the key, we say. We are saved because God chooses us. "In love He predestined us," says the Apostle Paul (Ephesians 1:4–5; cf. Romans 8:29–30). This is our gospel—we exalt the sovereignty of God, yet say little else. It's all God; faith and repentance, the human response to the gospel, rarely gets mentioned lest we diminish God's glory.

The result of this warp will be a form of fatalism known as hyper-Calvinism. Early Methodist evangelist Lorenzo Dow (1774–1834), meaning to satirize Calvinism, coined this ditty:

You can but you can't;
You will but you won't;
You're damned if you do, and
You're damned if you don't.

The distortion he mocks is not Calvinism but hyper-Calvinism, actually misnamed hyper-*Calvinism* because it's not Calvinism at all. It's fatalism. It's "mono causal fatalism," as it's been called. So-called hyper-Calvinists push the logic of election beyond the bounds of Scripture, resolving the tension between divine sovereignty and human responsibility in favor of the latter and at the expense of the former. As a consequence they deny that the gospel should be offered indiscriminately to all. Rather, Christ should only be offered to those in whom there were signs that the Holy Spirit was at work. When William Carey (1761–1834), father of the Modern Missionary Movement, first presented his idea of world evangelization to a group of ministers, one of them is reported to have said,

> Young man, sit down. When God pleases to convert the heathen, He will do it without your aid or mine.[1]

This is a fatalistic denial of human responsibility and an irresponsible failure to use God-appointed means. This error breeds passivity and false security. One misunderstands who one is and what is required in relation to God. Yet some so-called Calvinists have fallen into it by reducing the gospel to election without maintaining the biblical balance of human responsibility.

Regeneration

What happens if the gospel is reduced to being "born again," that is, to regeneration, or what the Westminster Confession calls the "effectual call"? Regeneration, like election, is crucial. Jesus told Nicodemus, "You must be born again" (John 3:1ff; cf. 2 Corinthians 5:17; Titus 3:5). Yet does regeneration stand on its own? Can the gospel be reduced to this? A few decades ago this was exactly what happened. Billy Graham preached the new birth in his crusades beginning in the late 1940s and even wrote a book entitled, *How to be Born Again* (1977), summarizing his message. Charles Colson penned *Born Again* (1976), an account of his conversion. Jimmy Carter was identified as

America's first "born again" President, and 1976 was labeled "The Year of the Evangelical." Thousands were urged to come forward, to sign a card or pray a prayer and decide to be "born again" and be saved. Well-meaning enthusiasts thought unless every sermon called sinners to be "born again" the gospel wasn't being preached. Many people were soundly converted in the 60s and 70s, the heyday of what might be called "decisional regeneration." This is not to be denied. However, other necessary responses such as repentance, commitment, and surrender to Christ were neglected. The doctrine of the "carnal," that is, unchanged "Christian" began to emerge as an explanation for the large numbers of "born again" but worldly "believers." Discipleship and obedience had become optional while assurance was assumed and salvation guaranteed because one was "born again." The gospel got warped. Christian identity got warped. The "believer" was one who made a decision that involved no deeper commitment than the decision itself. Decision was vital. Gospel preaching became monotonous and routine because every message was the same: "be born again." It was the same because that was *the* gospel.

Reconciliation

Reconciliation is not a regular element in the standard *ordo*, but it is an item in an expanded *ordo*, when additional elements of our salvation are elaborated. What happens when "reconciliation" becomes the whole gospel? Reconciliation is crucial. We are alienated from God and have been since the fall of Adam and Eve. Jesus reconciles us to God (Romans 5:10–14). We call the unbelieving to be reconciled to God (2 Corinthians 5:20). We tell them, rightly, that they can know God, and know Him *personally*. Yet when reconciliation, or "having a personal relationship with Jesus," becomes the dominant gospel motif, when it becomes the *whole* gospel, trouble results. Michael Horton and the ministry of White Horse Inn repeatedly have pointed out that "a personal relationship with Jesus" is language nowhere found in the Bible. When relational language stands alone, it inevitably distorts the gospel. What Jesus has accomplished out there, objectively, through the cross becomes less important, and my subjective experience, what is happening in my heart, becomes everything. Atonement, blood sacrifice, and penal substitution are pushed into the back seat. As with "born again," faith, repentance, commitment fade as one is led in prayer to establish a "personal relationship with Christ," there for the asking, presumably without any need for repentance or an atoning sacrifice. This is how they understand their Christian identity. Lots of folks speak of their "personal relationship" with God who have never faced their sins, never repented, and never submitted to the rule of Christ the King. Yet, they have a "personal relationship." Jesus is their friend. That is the crucial thing.

Adoption

In the 1990s adoption became the thing. It was seen as the key to everything Christian. Anyone who has read the *Westminster Confession of Faith* or J. I. Packer's chapter entitled, "Sons of God" in *Knowing God*, will know the crucial role that adoption plays in living the Christian life.[2] One can hardly overstate it. It's the key to prayer, to obedience, to assurance, to understanding adversity, to a familial understanding of our relationships with other believers, and so on. Yet some *did* overstate it. The "Sonship Movement" had gained a full head of steam by the mid-1990s. Its emphasis on adoption was helpful for many, many people. Yet for some, "Sons of God" became the Christian's whole identity. Lacking the balancing identities of "sinners" and "servants," our Father in heaven was transformed into an indulgent Daddy. "I'm a child of the King," the tiny-tot version of sonship, became the theme song of Sunday School. The whole motivation for the Christian life became gratitude to our Father. Never could He be displeased with us. Whenever He looked at us He only ever saw Jesus His Son. How then could He ever be disappointed with us? Keswick-like noises were heard emerging from this movement, urging that the believer need never strive to please the Father, or to secure His favor, or receive His blessing. Not quite "Let go and let God," but almost. Regardless of our behavior, we were assured that we retained the status quo of full Fatherly approval. I am God's child. Period. Result? Whole categories of motivation for Christians disappeared as well as whole categories of biblical approaches to pastoral problems. Rewards? Irrelevant. Punishments? Never. Judgment day? Doesn't apply. Fear? Don't be absurd. Zeal for holiness? For God's glory? Hadn't thought of it. Anyone preaching these themes, or duty, or responsibility, was accused of not preaching the gospel.

Justification

Finally in the 2000s justification rose to the top. Of course justification is crucial. It is at the heart of the gospel (see Ephesians 2:8–9; Romans 4:1–5). *Sola fide* is a principle that may never be compromised without giving up the gospel itself (Galatians 1:6). When straying movements emerged known as the "New Perspective on Paul" and "Federal Vision," or "Auburn Avenue," they rightly were sharply rebutted. The importance of justification is not at issue for us. The issue is, is justification the whole gospel? Is my identity as one who is justified my entire identity? The answer for some is yes. It swallows up everything. Sanctification becomes merely a matter of contemplating one's justification. Stumbled? Fallen into sin? Backslidden? Heaven forbid, don't preach law. Third use? No, no. What's needed is more gospel. Only the gospel, ever *more* gospel, narrowly defined as justification, motivates us. Everything else is unhelpful, discarded as law and unworthy. Ugly words like holiness, law, obedience, exhortation, duty, fear, warnings, and discipline fade into the sunset. All one need do to rise from the mire of sin is recall one's justification. Period. I am justified. This is my identity. This is in many ways adoption revisited (see above), with most of the same unhealthy imbalances. Looking to the cross is certainly the *first* thing that we should do, even the *primary* thing we should do. But the *only* thing? To propose such a strategy is to render meaningless great swathes of the New Testament pastoral practice. It is also to invite carnality and spiritual complacency. I am, as Luther insisted, *simul jus et peccator,* at once justified *and sinner.*

Sanctification, Glorification

There have been other movements. Several mid-nineteenth century groups elevated sanctification to the pinnacle, and various "holiness" movements resulted. "This is the will of God, your sanctification" (1 Thessalonians 4:30). Holy living is vital. "You shall be holy, for I am holy" (1 Peter 1:16). There is that "holiness without which no one will see the Lord" (Hebrews 12:14). Stressing holiness is vital. Yet they went on to say that we can have total victory over sin if only we would. Enough of the "woe is me" gloom, what they disparaged as "worm" theology and "miserable sinner" defeatism.

However, sanctification, standing alone, inevitably results in moralism or perfectionism, or both, which is where most of these movements, even whole denominations, ended up. "Entire sanctification" was earnestly pursued, especially by Wesleyans. Believers were said to have the capacity to live without conscious or deliberate sin through intense consecration and effort. The definition of sin was thereby dumbed-down (conscious acts) and the concept of holiness externalized (evident in visible spiritual disciplines such as prayer and Bible reading, and in plain dress and abstinence from "worldly" pleasures) and takes on a legalistic tone. The grace of God, union with Christ in His resurrection (Romans 6:1ff), the enabling power of the Holy Spirit either receded or were understood mechanically. Anyone schooled on the Campus Crusade "bird book," with the concept of "spiritual breathing," and the promise of victory over sin through correct technique and effort, will know the maddening frustration of perfectionism in any of its various forms. B. B. Warfield (1851–1921), the brilliant theologian of Old Princeton, became so exercised about the "higher life" and "victorious life" teaching that he wrote over 1000 pages against it in the waning years of his career.[3]

There have even been glorification movements, what theologians might call a "realized" or "over-realized eschatology." "Glorified," as in "these He also glorified," is in the past tense (Romans 8:30). It's done. This means that we are secure. This security needs to be taught. Our salvation to the point of its completion in glorification is an accomplished fact. The "golden chain" of salvation, from election to glorification, cannot be broken. Yet these movements went on to say we are glorified now, meaning we can have it all *now*: health, wealth, freedom from sin's power, *now*. Shipwrecked on the rocks of reality (along with its close friends, the sanctification movements), the reality of poverty, pain, disappointment, and struggle is where these "glorification" movements have terminated.

Typically these various "warps," these "Potato Head" movements arise for the best of motives. Concerns grow for a perceived lopsidedness in the formulation of the gospel being widely expressed. A new emphasis is stressed, be it election, regeneration, reconciliation, justification, adoption, sanctification, or glorification. Legalism? We'll preach grace. Exclusively. License? We'll preach law and more law. "Worm" theology? We'll preach entire sanctification, even perfection. Dead formalism? We'll preach a personal relationship with God. Moralism? We'll preach supernatural rebirth and justification. Fatalism? We'll preach the use of means. Manipulative methods? We'll preach the sovereignty of God. However, too often in the process the new theme also becomes lopsided. One Potato Head is exchanged for another, with destructive consequences for the Christian's expectation, his self-concept, his identity.

Gospel truths are not meant to stand alone. "False proportions in our doctrine are the beginning of false doctrine itself,"[4] Packer warns. Gospel truths need gospel proportions. Together they form a beautiful, balanced, nuanced whole. Isolate election from the rest and expect to slide into fatalism. Isolate regeneration or reconciliation and expect the historic and objective events of the cross, what Jesus did outside of us and for us, to fade in favor of the subjective and experiential. Isolate adoption and justification and expect the ethical dimension of the gospel to get short-changed. Isolate sanctification and expect a moralistic legalism to result. And isolate and temporalize glorification and one's expectations of bliss in this world may be raised to a level that can never be met, and the gospel will be discredited in the process. Beware of those who play a single note over and over again. "A half-truth masquerading as the whole truth becomes a complete untruth," Packer warns.[5] We need a whole Christ and a whole gospel if we are to receive a whole salvation, and *if we are to understand our identity in Christ.*

David Powlison recently wrote three wonderful articles on sanctification for the *Journal of Biblical Counseling.* He summarizes well our concern: "Whenever one very good truth is exalted into the only truth that matters, ministry suffers. And when ministry suffers, it hinders the actual sanctification of the saints, sufferers, and sinners that we are."[6]

2. Our Human Identity

Then God said, "Let us make man in our image, after our likeness. And let them have dominion over the fish of the sea and over the birds of the heavens and over the livestock and over all the earth and over every creeping thing that creeps on the earth." So God created man in his own image, in the image of God he created him; male and female he created them. (Genesis 1:26–27)

Christian preachers and authors for some time now have focused on Christian believers' "identity in Christ," rightly understanding that if some other identity dominates the outlook of a believer (vocation, accomplishments, family, social status), it will smother their spiritual life. More recently, identity has become an important topic in wider cultural conversations. The politics of intersectionality have heightened, for some, the importance of race, gender, and sexual orientation. "Identity politics" have introduced a new tribalism in our cultural conversations as group identity has trumped political philosophy in forming political alliances. Today we are being assured that we may now identify anywhere along the spectrum of genders outside the "binary" of male and female. We have entered into what secular commentators have called the "transgender moment." The philosophical basis of this "moment" is the separating of "sex," one's anatomy, from "gender," one's sense of self. One might be a man anatomically but a woman in actuality, hence, a woman trapped in the body of a man. A biological man may identify as a woman and a biological woman may identify as a man and be regarded as such by society. Unprecedented confusion has resulted. Biological boys who identify as girls are being allowed to use girls restrooms and locker room facilities. Transgender girls (that is, biological boys) are dominating girls/women's athletic events. Feminists understandably warn that if biological males can be reclassified as females and counted as such in boardrooms and professions, as well as athletics, the gains made by women in recent decades are put at risk. The transgender movement, they argue, may become the back door through which male dominance is reasserted, as biological males take the positions and win the rewards that would have gone to biological females. This cultural discussion and the conflict it has spawned makes it all the more urgent that Christians correctly understand their true identity. Who am I? What am I? Given who and what I am, what is expected of me, and what is best for me?

Before we delve into the details of our identity as Christians (our main theme), we must first establish its foundation in our identity as human beings. Our Christian identity assumes and builds upon our identity in God's created order. Contemporary ethical debates often betray fundamental disagreements over human identity and destiny. We do not agree with the unbelieving world about who we are, how we got here, and where we are going. Hence, consensus is impossible. Are we to identify primarily upward with the angels or downward with the animals? Is there something "special" about us individually and collectively, or is thinking that we are "special" the main cause behind our social, environmental, and ecological problems? These are the kinds of questions we must resolve if we are to attain a full understanding of our identity first as humans, and then as Christians.

Created by God

The first characteristic of humanity is that we are created by God. "Then God said, 'Let us make man [...] So God created man'" (Genesis 1:26–27). We are not here by chance. We are not the product of blind forces that somehow erupted in the universe. Rather, we were created and placed here by an all-powerful and all-wise God. The God who created us is (to state the obvious) a Creator. The Bible begins with Genesis 1 so that we might know the source of all that exists. God said, "Let there be" and there was. "For he spoke and it came to be; he commanded, and it stood firm" (Psalm 33:9). He consulted no one. He required no advisors. He needed no helpers (Isaiah 40:14). The universe in its vastness, its enormous energy, its extraordinary complexity, and its strikingly nuanced order, is a product of the deliberate, purposeful creative word of God.

Calvin's classic work, *The Institutes of the Christian Religion*, begins by asserting that all knowledge consists of two parts: the knowledge of God and of ourselves. Furthermore, he argues that we cannot know ourselves unless we first know God. Self-knowledge begins with knowing that God made the world I inhabit and that He made me. I was made and placed in the world to fulfil His purposes. He is the potter and I am but clay (Romans 9:21). I was formed not to do with my life whatever I wish. My life is not "my life." I belong to my Maker. I am accountable to Him. If I think of myself as autonomous, or free to do whatever I want, I misconstrue the meaning of my existence. I was made to honor, serve, worship, and glorify God. I was created by God for God.

This means I have a purpose. I was placed here for a reason. My life is not meaningless. I am not an accident. I am not the chance product of a blind universe. My life has intention. My "chief end" in the language of *The Shorter Catechism*, or my primary purpose, is to glorify God and enjoy Him forever.

> For from him and through him and to him are all things. To him be glory forever. Amen. (Romans 11:36)

"Created by God" also means that the foundational elements of our identity are not chosen but given. We are modern people; we did not choose *when* we were born. We are family people; we did not choose *to whom* we were born. We were born in a given nation or region; we did not choose *where* we were born. We were born either male or female; we did not choose our sex or with what anatomy we were born. We are ethnic people; we did not choose our race or ethnicity. All of these are givens. All of these are unalterable. All of these contribute to who we are. Contrary to modern notions of the self, we are not able to make of ourselves whatever we wish ourselves to be. The when, to whom, where, and what we are were all God-given and God-determined, not chosen. This is a crucial element in our self-understanding, as we will see.

Image of God

Genesis 1 teaches me not only that I was created by God, but I was created with a particular design. "Let us make man in our image, after our likeness" (Genesis 1:26). Humanity is set apart from the rest of creation as image-bearers. Man is "a little lower than the angels" and given dominion over the plant and animal kingdoms (Genesis 1:26; Psalm 8:6–8). As God's vice-regent, man alone is both to care for creation and rule over it. Because I am made in God's image, my life has dignity. My life is sacred. My life has importance. I bear the image and likeness of God.

My neighbors also are image-bearers. Their lives are sacred. Their lives have dignity. They are my equal. This has everything to do with the regard I am to have for them. Because their lives are sacred, *God requires the ultimate penalty of those who would unjustly take the life of another (Genesis 9:4).* Because they bear God's image, God forbids that I pretend to bless Him with the same mouth with which I might curse them (James 3:10). All human life is sacred from conception to natural death. All human beings are endowed with an essential dignity and equality that all must respect. People are not trash. People are not insects to step upon. People are not animals upon which I might ride and into which I might dig my spurs. Honor and respect is due to all as image-bearers.

Given this essential dignity and sanctity of all human life, everything that is contrary to that essential dignity, sanctity and equality should be avoided. There is that which is fitting and appropriate to human nature and that which is "contrary to nature," as the Apostle Paul puts it (Romans 1:26, NASB). We shall examine this in greater detail in a moment. Meanwhile, I am to know that my life is valuable and purposeful. I am designed by God as an image-bearer with His specific intentions for me in view.

Our bodies

Our bodies are an essential part of our identity. The body is not something external to us. It is not a prison in which our souls, our true selves are trapped. It is not a barrier to self-expression to be overcome. What do tattooing, body piercing, blue hair, and transgender surgery have in common? They all view the body as a potential, not actual tool or vehicle of self-expression. The body itself, the body alone, it is thought, is inadequate to be such. It is external to the self. It is detached from the person who inhabits it. It fails to inform the soul. It fails to communicate who and what the person is. Consequently, a self-revelatory message or image may be tattooed onto the body; the body may be pierced and decorated to give expression to one's distinctive identity; the hair may be died an unnatural color to define who the person is, his or her uniqueness or distinctiveness; sexual organs may be removed and reconfigured to more perfectly match the body with the true inner self, one's true identity. The body itself, many assume, does not communicate identity; it is merely a billboard onto which the individual stamps his or her subjective sense of identity.

The Bible views these matters quite differently. It forbids physical disfigurement by tattooing and scarring as means by which one establishes identity, whether tribal or otherwise (Leviticus 19:28; cf 21:6; Deuteronomy 14:1–2). Human beings are a psycho-physical unity. Salvation, even sanctification includes not just the spirit and soul, but also the body (1 Thessalonians 5:23). The members or parts of our bodies are transformed from slaves of unrighteousness to slaves of righteousness (Romans 6:12–16, 19). Our bodies are "members of Christ" (1 Corinthians 6:15). Our bodies are "temple(s) of the Holy Spirit" (1 Corinthians 6:19). Our bodies are presented to God as living sacrifices (Romans 12:1–2). Our bodies will be raised up on the last day and we will continue eternally as embodied beings (Romans 8:10–11; 1 Corinthians 15:50–58; Philippians 13:20–21; 2 Corinthians 4:16–17). Our bodies are an essential part of human nature, and as such, must inform our sense of identity. It is vital that a Christian theology of the body be understood. Because we were created as embodied beings, our bodies as given are vehicles of genuine self-expression, informing our understanding of our true selves. Rather than barriers to self-discovery, they provide vital information for our true self-understanding, information that we disregard to our peril.

Male and female

"Male and female he created them" (Genesis 1:27). The terms "male" and "female" are the Hebrew terms for sexual distinction that apply to insects, animals, and humans. God did not merely make humanity man and woman, but male and female with purposefully distinct but complimentary sexual identities. He made us with male bodies and female bodies. The differences between male and female are deliberate. The differences are intended. The differences are designed. The differences are good. I am either a man or a woman. There is no third sex. When God created the woman, she was taken from the man and therefore shares his image and nature. She is defined as a helper, a companion for his solitude ("It is not good to be alone"), who is "meet" (KJV), that is, apt or suited to the man and the man to her as a woman (Genesis 2:18). She is designed for him and he for her (1 Corinthians 11:8–12). They complement each other. Their physiology and their anatomy— the distinctive sexual organs of men and women—make this obvious.

If I am male, then I have the characteristics that are distinctively male, what we call masculine. If I am female, I have distinctively female characteristics, what we call feminine. If I am male, I have a God-given capacity to father human life. I have as well the complimentary paternal characteristics that accompany that distinctive capacity. I have an instinct, a drive, and an enhanced physical capacity to guard, protect and provide for my offspring. If I am a female, I have a God-given capacity to birth and nourish human life—to mother. I also have the complimentary maternal characteristics that accompany that distinctive capacity. I have an instinct or a drive to bear and nurture my offspring, and a particular concern to ensure their safety, security, and provision.

All that we have described thus far is good and very good (Genesis 1:31). We apologize for none of it. God's design and intention is to be appreciated and celebrated. We are "fearfully and wonderfully made" (Psalm 139:14). When the Bible raises the question, "What is man that you are mindful of him [...] that you care for him?", a question raised by comparison with the majesty and glory of God (Psalm 8:1–4), the enthusiastic answer is,

> Yet you have made him a little lower than the heavenly beings and crowned him with glory and honor. You have given him dominion over the works of your hands; you have put all things under his feet (Psalm 8:5–6)

When we fully grasp the implications of our Maker's design, we find answers for a number of the questions that perplex our times. Putting things simply, the design of our bodies is to inform our minds regarding our Maker's intentions for us. Our thinking is to conform to created, physical reality. In this respect, biology is destiny. We are not to attempt to bend reality to our illusions. The body, we repeat, is not extrinsic to the person, to who we are. The body and our internal selves were not stuck together arbitrarily or accidentally. Our bodies are an essential part of our identity. To say otherwise is to demean the body and with it the entire material world. I am a man intended to fulfil the physical design of a man or a woman meant to fulfil the physical design of a woman. Let's be specific.

Sexual orientation

The sexual component of human nature is designed to be expressed in relation to the opposite sex. The argument of the Apostle Paul in Romans 1 is that erotic desire for a member of the same sex involves the exchange of the "natural relations" for the "unnatural" or that which is "contrary to nature" as God has designed it (Romans 1:26, NASB). These unnatural desires he terms "dishonorable passions" and "shameless acts" and things that "ought not to be done" (Romans 1:26–28). Homosexual acts are unnatural. Sodomy, and other unnatural practices, and their female equivalents are contrary to the physiological design as well as the biological meaning of sexual acts. Sexual organs are designed for pleasure, to be sure. Yet their biological function is procreational. When utilized in contexts that fail to honor that procreational design, they are corrupted (see Leviticus 18:22–23; 20:10–16; 1 Corinthians 6:9–10). Rod Dreher, in his provocative book *The Benedict Option*, is right to assert that "the legitimacy of our sexual desire is limited by the givenness of nature." There are forms of sexual expression that are contrary to, and degrading of human nature. Prostitution degrades both the seller and the customer. Polygamy degrades both the husband and his multiple wives. Sodomy degrades both the active and passive participants. Bestiality is inherently evil.

Who am I? I am a sexual being who is either male or female. To whom is my sexual desires to be directed? To a member of the opposite sex as our Maker's design indicates. If I were to find myself experiencing erotic desire toward members of the same sex, my response should be to mortify those desires, as is the case with all sinful desires, and seek to bring them in line with my Creator's plan (Romans 8:13). If I am a man, I am designed to be united to a woman. If I am a woman, I am designed to be united to a man. Aside from this other-sex union, I am to remain un-united altogether.

Gender identity

The increasing prevalence of, or at least popularizing of what has been called "gender dysphoria," also is answered by our Maker's design. The world has a deliberate unchanging design and nature. At 32 degrees F. water becomes ice. That reality has to be accommodated when we store liquids in our freezers. The earth's gravitational pull has to be accommodated when bridges and airplanes are built. Dreher again asks the right questions: "Is the natural world and its limits a given, or are we free to do with it whatever we desire?" There is a givenness to human design and nature which to fight against is sheer folly. Boys are not girls and girls are not boys. Christians need not worry that they might be the gender that is the opposite of that of their bodies. They are what their body is, male or female. Those who think that they are men trapped in the bodies of women, or women trapped in the bodies of men, should be urged to bring their minds into conformity with their bodies, not the other way around. Those who have likened "gender dysphoria" to anorexia surely are right. Girls who think they are fat while they dangerously approach starvation must be helped to perceive their bodies correctly.

It is estimated that anorexia affects nearly three million people globally and results in about 600 deaths annually. Celebrity victims include the pop star Pat Boone's daughter Debbie whose 1977 song, "You Light Up My Life" was number one on the top 40 chart for ten weeks, longer than any other song of the 1970s.

Her book *Starving for Attention* (1982) caused a sensation in the evangelical Christian world. However, it was Karen Carpenter, whom the Beatle's Paul McCartney called "the best female voice in the world" and Elton John called "one of the greatest voices of our lifetime," whose death at the age of 32 in 1983 brought the problem into focus. Both women identified themselves as overweight when in fact they were shockingly underweight. It should be obvious that the self-perceptions of anorexic girls must not be reinforced. Their self-identification as obese must not be affirmed. Anorexic girls may find it cruel when there is a lack of understanding and affirmation by parents and medical professionals, yet those who love them must be undaunted. Their condition is a matter of physical reality and their minds must be brought into conformity with that reality, lest tragedy result.

The same is true of "gender identity disorder" or what is also called "gender dysphoria." Those thus afflicted misperceive physical reality. They misperceive their own identity. To affirm their misperceptions is cruel and may lead to irreversible physical changes. Tragically, parents are consenting to their teenage daughters' desire for double mastectomies, hormone therapy, and reconstructive surgery. Doctors are surgically mutilating and reshaping body parts and prescribing powerful drugs in attempts to alter the unalterable. These drastic steps have rightly been identified with malpractice, whether parental or medical. Both are fighting against the God-given reality of maleness and femaleness found in every cell in the human body. We are either xx or xy in all one trillion of our cells and our sexual organs are either male or female. This is why "sex change" is impossible. The body may be mutilated. Organs may be restructured. Yet one remains what biology, anatomy, genetics, and chromosomes say we are.

God's design of our bodies and each cell that comprises our bodies is the key to our gender identity. Who am I? I am one who was created by God in His image, as a man or a woman, in order to fulfil the specific purposes of my design as a man or a woman.

Marriage

Male and female image-bearers were designed for sexual union that is permanent and procreational. Returning to Genesis, we read again of the Creator's design:

> And God blessed them. And God said to them, "Be fruitful and multiply and fill the earth and subdue it," (Genesis 1:28a)

> Therefore a man shall leave his father and his mother and hold fast to his wife, and they shall become one flesh. (Genesis 2:24)

God made humanity for marriage, and marriage, by definition, is a procreative union. Marriage is a procreative union that consummates the consensual commitment of a man and a woman. "A man" shall have "his wife." From the beginning, marriage was not meant to be polygamous or homosexual. God did not give Adam multiple women but brought one to him. The same can be said of Eve. Homosexual marriage is as impossible as square circles. "Be fruitful and multiply," they are commanded. The man and the woman become "one flesh" in marriage, a union designed to bear the fruit of children and fulfil the command.

Marriage is also designed to be permanent. Jesus draws this further lesson from God's original design by prohibiting divorce. He appeals to what was "from the beginning" over against what Moses permitted "because of the hardness of heart" (Matthew 19:8). He identifies God's will as expressed by his design in these words: "What therefore God has joined together, let not man separate." (Matthew 19:6b)

God made us as sexual beings. He also created a context within his gift of sexual expression is to take place: marriage. All pre-marital and extra-marital sexual activity is forbidden. They are contrary to our divinely given design and is contrary to human flourishing. Ultimately they harm those who indulge in it.

Conclusions

I have learned quite a lot about myself based on my created human identity alone. I have learned that I was made by God and for God; that I was made in the image of God; that my life is sacred; that I share an essential dignity and equality with all my fellow humans; that my body is a crucial element in my identity; that I was made either male or female; and that I was made for marriage to a member of the opposite sex, or not to marry at all. Whereas tragic confusion has been introduced to society through the normalizing of deviations from these norms, I need not share in the confusion. Because I know that God has made me, I know His will for me simply by consulting the design of my body. Insofar as my desires lead me in another direction, I know that those desires are to be mortified and my thinking brought into conformity with my Maker's benevolent design.

3. Our Fallen Identity

Clearly we have not said all that need to be said about our human identity. We have assumed but not yet accounted for the obviously broken condition of humanity. The image of God has been marred to the point of obliteration. English poet William Wordsworth (1770–1850) wrote beautifully of the ruins of Tintern Abbey, the 12th century cathedral ruins found in Wales. A visit to the site makes an indelible impression. One sees greatness, yet one also sees ruins. One sees remnants of grand structures yet they have crumbled beyond repair, if not beyond recognition. So it is with humanity. We retain our essential dignity, sanctity, and equality as image-bearers. Our capacity for communication, for rationality, for creativity, and for dominion are visible and admirable. Yet also unmistakable is our capacity for cruelty, for perversity, for idolatry, and for self-destruction. Human history is a study of scientific, artistic, musical, and literary achievement, as well as one of continuous lies, moral degradation, war, violence, and oppression.

Fallen

What must I know about myself? That I am part of a human race that is corrupt both by nature and in practice. We are a "fallen" people. Our ancient ancestors fell, the well-known story of which is recorded in Genesis 3.

> Now the serpent was more crafty than any other beast of the field that the Lord God had made. He said to the woman, "Did God actually say, 'You shall not eat of any tree in the garden'?" And the woman said to the serpent, "We may eat of the fruit of the trees in the garden, but God said, "You shall not eat of the fruit of the tree that is in the midst of the garden, neither shall you touch it, lest you die.'" But the serpent said to the woman, "You will not surely die. For God knows that when you eat of it your eyes will be opened, and you will be like God, knowing good and evil." So when the woman saw that the tree was good for food, and that it was a delight to the eyes, and that the tree was to be desired to make one wise, she took of its fruit and ate, and she also gave some to her husband who was with her, and he ate. (Genesis 3:1–6)

God warned that "in the day that you eat of [the tree of the knowledge of good and evil], you surely shall die" (Genesis 2:17). So it was that "sin came into the world […] and death through sin" (Romans 5:12). Adam and Eve died spiritually immediately, and the process of their physical death began. Through them, sin and death was transmitted to their descendants. "Because of one man's trespass, death reigned through that one man" (Romans 5:17). "By the one man's disobedience the many were made sinners" (Romans 5:19).

Inclined to evil

What must I know about myself? That by nature I am bent towards evil. The Lord Jesus teaches that we, by nature, "love the darkness rather than the light" (John 3:19–20). We always choose evil or good for evil motives. The Apostle Paul provides this climactic summary of the human condition in Romans 3:

> None is righteous, no, not one; no one understands; no one seeks for God. All have turned aside; together they have become worthless; no one does good, not even one. (Romans 3:10b–12)

The Apostle is categorical—"none is righteous," "no one seeks for God," "no one does good, not even one." The fall explains humanity's ruins. The fall explains my outbursts of anger, my lust, my gluttony, my petty envies and jealousies and covetousness, my cruelty, my selfishness, self-centeredness, and self-absorption. It includes any wayward thoughts, motives, words, and deeds. My fallen nature asserting itself in a fallen world means I cannot trust my mind, my emotions or my volitions. I cannot trust my self-perceptions. I cannot trust my passions, my desires, or my dreams. I cannot rely on my reasoning, my arguments, or my explanations. Self-deception is a constant danger. The Apostle Paul warns us,

> Let no one deceive himself. If anyone among you thinks that he is wise in this age, let him become a fool that he may become wise. (1 Corinthians 3:18)

The self-deceived "wise in this age." They rely on human reason alone, and as a result, they err. They fail to rely on the wisdom of God, which is foolishness to them (1 Corinthians 1:18ff). We must be fools according to the standard of the world if we are to become wise. "For the wisdom of this world is folly with God" (1 Corinthians 3:19; cf 1:20, 25; 2:6, 7, 13–16). "Do not be deceived," we are warned repeatedly (Romans 16:18; 1 Corinthians 6:9; Galatians 6:7; Ephesians 5:6; 2 Thessalonians 2:3; James 1:6; 1 John 3:7). Why? Because we are vulnerable to deception. The devil himself is a deceiver and his agents are deceivers (2 Corinthians 11:3; 1 Timothy 3:13; Titus 1:10; 1 John

2:26; 2 John 7; Revelation 12:9; 13:14; 18:23; 19:20; 20:3, 8, 10). Yet, worst of all perhaps, is self-deception. Listen to these biblical warnings:

> For if anyone thinks he is something, when he is nothing, he deceives himself. (Galatians 6:3)

> But be doers of the word, and not hearers only, deceiving yourselves. (James 1:22)

> If anyone thinks he is religious and does not bridle his tongue but deceives his heart, this person's religion is worthless. (James 1:26)

> If we say we have no sin, we deceive ourselves, and the truth is not in us. (1 John 1:8)

Taking these warnings together, our spiritual and moral self-assessments may tragically err. We are surrounded by human and superhuman deceivers who design our destruction. Our own capacity for self-evaluation and self-diagnosis and self-assessment is disastrously flawed. We cannot trust our own fallen and corrupt judgment. Yet this is exactly what we are prone to do. We are tempted to believe that what we feel, what we sense, what we perceive about ourselves cannot be wrong and must be right. Our real selves, we think, our authentic selves are what we conceive ourselves to be. On the contrary, if I truly know myself, I know that I am an unreliable mess of error and misperception.

Hostile to God

My aversion to the light of truth and righteousness ultimately means aversion to God. Hence, "no one seeks for God." Indeed, we are described by the Bible as "haters of God" (Romans 1:30) and "hostile" towards God (Romans 8:7). We flee from God, suppressing our sense of the divine, exchanging "the truth of God for a lie and worship(ing) and serv(ing) the creature rather than the Creator" (Romans 1:25; cf 1:18–24). Consequently, the condition of alienation exists between humanity and God. We were made to know God, to love God, and to enjoy fellowship with Him. Instead we are "enemies" of God and consequently "helpless" (Romans 5:6, 8). Our souls are hungry, thirsty, and empty. We need the Bread of Life (John 6:35). We need Living Water (John 4:10; 7:37–38). Only as we hunger and thirst for righteousness can we be satisfied (Matthew 5:6).

The desperately needed reconciliation with our Maker is exactly what Jesus has accomplished for us, the Apostle Paul explains:

> For if while we were enemies we were reconciled to God by the death of his Son, much more, now that we are reconciled, shall we be saved by his life. More than that, we also rejoice in God through our Lord Jesus Christ, through whom we have now received reconciliation. (Romans 5:10–11)

This reconciliation is transformative. We are "born again" or "born of the Spirit" (John 3:3–8). The repair of our faculties of thinking, feeling, and choosing begins. We become a "new creation" in Christ. We become new people with new identities. "The old has passed away" and "the new has come." Our thinking, feeling, and choosing now submits to God's word and His unerring wisdom. The journey of true and reliable self-discovery now begins. "All this," the Apostle continues, "is from God, who through Christ reconciled us to himself" (2 Corinthians 5:17–21)

*   *   *   *   *

This new identity is what we will now explore. We do so

realizing that we are profoundly damaged and needy. We do so looking only to Christ for healing and repair. The Bible uses a variety of metaphors by which to understand what Christ has done for us. Keeping these metaphors in balance is our first challenge in establishing Christian identity.

II. Our Primary Identity

4. Behaviour and Identity

If anyone else thinks he has reason for confidence in the flesh, I have more: circumcised on the eighth day, of the people of Israel, of the tribe of Benjamin, a Hebrew of Hebrews; as to the law, a Pharisee; as to zeal, a persecutor of the church; as to righteousness under the law, blameless. But whatever gain I had, I counted as loss for the sake of Christ. Indeed, I count everything as loss because of the surpassing worth of knowing Christ Jesus my Lord. For his sake I have suffered the loss of all things and count them as rubbish, in order that I may gain Christ (Philippians 3:4–8)

The Apostle Paul is rebutting certain "Judaizers" who teach that salvation is by faith in Christ *plus*. Their message was that faith in Christ is necessary for salvation, but they insisted one must also keep the ceremonial requirements of the law. One must be circumcised (Acts 15:1; Galatians 5:1ff). One must observe the dietary laws (Colossians 2:16, 21; 1 Timothy 4:2–5; Romans 14:2–3). One must keep the calendar of holy days (Colossians 2:16; Galatians 4:10–11; Romans 14:5–6). One must follow the cleansing ordinances (Romans 14:14–15). The Apostle calls them the "false circumcision" (Philippians 3:2 NASB). He rebuts them in verse 9 with what has been called the whole book of Romans in one verse:

and be found in him, not having a righteousness of my own
that comes from the law, but that which comes through faith
in Christ, the righteousness from God that depends on faith
(Philippians 3:9)

In the course of building his argument, he identifies those
accomplishments and characteristics in which we tend to
place our confidence before both God and man. These tend
to overlap. The accomplishments and characteristics about
which we boast and by which we establish our social pecking
order—in relation to our fellows—surely commend us to
God as well, the thinking goes. The Apostle points out that
he had bloodlines. He was of the people of Israel, the tribe of
Benjamin, "a Hebrew of Hebrews" (Philippians 3:5). He had
religious stature which also meant social stature in a civilization
which esteemed religious observance: circumcised on the
eighth day, a Pharisee, that is, among the religious elite, and
a "blameless" observer of the Law (Philippians 3:6). He was
educated by Gamaliel, the leading rabbi of the day (Acts 22:3),
and a Roman citizen in a world in which such citizenship
was highly sought (Acts 22:28). What does all that social and
religious and educational and professional accomplishment
and status amount to for the Christian? Does it define us? Do
we boast of it? Does it commend us to God? If it does not, is
it worth much even in relation to man? The Apostle says it is
as nothing, "rubbish," compared to the "surpassing worth" of
knowing and serving and honoring Christ Jesus as Lord.

Years ago a promising young sportsman was identified as
the next dominant multi-sport athlete. Through lower and
middle school he excelled all his rivals in whatever competition
he entered. He was popular with the boys and girls alike.
High school coaches eagerly awaited his arrival. As he stood
on the cusp of athletic achievement, he was cut down by a

serious injury. Then another. And another. His dreams were shattered. So also was his identity. Who was he? He used to know who he was. He was an athlete, *the* athlete. He was popular. He knew where he belonged. He use to know where he fit in, where he was secure, atop the teenage social pyramid. No more. Thereafter he watched others achieve. Athletes he once dominated came to excel, as he watched on the sideline. They progressed. He was left behind.

He began to look for a place to settle. A crisis of *identity* spawned a crisis of *belonging*. The athletes were busy with their teams, and had little time for him. He cast about for a place to associate. Where could he hang out? He wasn't brilliant. He couldn't keep pace with the scholars. He wasn't a musician or an actor. He wasn't a "nerd." He wouldn't fit in with any of them. Where would he be accepted?

There was one place. The "partiers," as they are benignly (and misleadingly) called, would take him in. The only qualification was that one had to party with them. Party-up, and you're in. All dopers and drinkers were welcome. Slowly he began to hang out with them. First this happened only during school hours. As he became more comfortable with them, and they with him, it extended to after school hours, and, inevitably, to their after school activities. First he began to drink. Then over drink. Then drunkenness became the norm.

Then he began to experiment with drugs. First a single puff. Then periodic indulgence. Before long he became a regular. He even would leave school grounds at lunch time with his buddies and smoke a joint or two, returning to class on time but with bloodshot eyes and traces of burnt hemp clinging to his clothing. Compounding the tragedy of this young man is this:

he was reared in a Christian home and in a strong Christian church.

What happened? The failure of our mythical young man is multi-layered, and blame can be placed in several areas. However, one important element is that of identity. How did he identify himself during his years of popularity? As an athlete. What is the problem with this? An identity rooted in the transient is itself transient. Once a transient identity is uprooted, by injury, by financial loss, by divorce, by social rejection, one is "at sea," adrift and vulnerable.

What is our primary identity? It is that we are disciples of Christ. We are Christians. Read the introductions to the Apostles' letters—how do they identify themselves? It is always in relation to Christ, either as an Apostle of Christ Jesus (see the introductions to 1 & 2 Corinthians; Ephesians; Colossians; 1 & 2 Timothy; 1 & 2 Peter), a bond-servant of Christ (see the introductions to Romans, Philippians, Titus, James, Jude, 2 Peter), or a prisoner of Christ (see the introduction to Philemon). The Apostles are *defined* by their relation to Christ. They retain the other components of their identities. For example, the Apostle Paul is a Roman citizen, and will appeal to Caesar for his rights (Acts 25:11). He is a Pharisee, and will appeal to fellow Pharisees for support (Acts 23:6). He will appeal to his worldly identity and achievements when he needs to do so, especially for the sake of the gospel (2 Corinthians 11:22; Philippians 3:4–6). However, his primary identification is that he is a Christian disciple. The rest, his nationality, his group identity, his scholarship, his other admired achievements are all expendable. He regards them as "rubbish" (Philippians 3:4–8). "Who am I?" is one crucial question that I must answer if I am to realize the fullness of the Christian life.

Identity and behavior

Identity is often confused with *image*. Our civilization is highly obsessed with image. Social media has aggravated what was already an accelerating trend. We have a huge *cosmetic* industry designed to enhance our image. We have a vast *fashion* industry dedicated to cultivating our image. We have a *medical* community that will surgically remove the signs of aging, removing wrinkles and lumps and spots and providing various enhancements. *Social media* now allows us selectively to show the world what our life consists of: only and always that which is fun, exciting, hip, and cool. For many people, image is their identity. They define themselves in terms of the image they project, though every element of that image (age, beauty, wealth, activities) is external and superficial and ultimately unsatisfying.

Obviously, our concern is not with *image*, but identity. Who am I? I am a disciple of Christ. I am a believer. I am a Christian.

Because I am a disciple of Christ, I am called "to walk in a manner worthy of the Lord," that is, conduct life in a way that is consistent with, or compatible with, who Christ is and who we are in Christ (Colossians 1:10). This identity defines who I am and consequently what I believe, how I behave, and even where I belong.

Otto Friedrich (1929–1995), in his book *Blood and Iron*, tells about an incident in his father's childhood in Germany. When the time came for his tonsils to be removed the doctor approached him with his shiny stainless steel surgical scissors and asked, "Now are you a brave German boy or are you somebody who cries and has to be put to sleep?" "What did you answer?" Friedrich asked his father squeamishly. "I said I was a brave German boy and that was that."[1] Identity, as we can see, has much to say about behavior.

Winston Churchill's matchless speeches of the World War II era brilliantly invoked identity as a motivation for resistance. After the Munich Pact (1938), when Neville Chamberlain's tragic appeasement of Hitler had sacrificed Czechoslovakia for the sake of "peace in our time," he urged a recovery of the "moral strength and martial vigor" that would enable Britain to stand against moral evil, as it had so often in "olden times." Had Britain not stood alone against the Spanish Armada, against Napoleon, and the Kaiser? "We shall never surrender" was an invocation of British identity, British courage, British determination to resist the forces of tyranny. We are British, and this is what we have always done, and what we will now do, whatever the cost.

Less eloquently, yet appealing to the same principle, Nikki Giovanni, an official at Virginia Tech University, undaunted by the campus massacre in April 2007, repeated time and again, "We are Virginia Tech!" She invoked identity. Because we are, she urged, we will not allow this tragedy to defeat us, define us, or deflect us from our mission.

The crisis of identity, we repeat, is also a crisis of belonging. Who am I? I am first and foremost a disciple of Christ, "in Christ" (a favorite New Testament designation). Where, then, do I *belong*? I am a citizen of heaven (Philippians 3:20), a member of the body of Christ (1 Corinthians 12; Romans 12), the church, the separated people of God (2 Corinthians 6:14–18). Who are we? We are a holy people called out of darkness and into God's marvelous light (1 Peter 2:9–12), mocked (1 Peter 4:3–5), and hated by the world (John 15:18–25). We are fools for Christ's sake (1 Corinthians 4:9–13), who in turn reject friendship with the world (James 4:4–5), who love not the world (1 John 2:15–17), who have fixed our minds on things above and not things below (Colossians 3:2; 2 Corinthians 4:18), who love our neighbors, love our enemies, and love one another (Matthew 5:38–48). All of this (and much, much more) is wrapped up in our identity. Because of what Christ has done we have a new group to which we belong. We are the people of God. We stand in a long line of heroes and martyrs of faith, a "great cloud of witnesses" (Hebrews 11:1–12:1). Our identity plants us among a particular people and dictates a way of life consistent with our leader (Jesus) and His people all through the ages.

On the eve of USC–Notre Dame football games the ghosts of heroes and heroic exploits are resurrected in pep rallies, to remind present athletes and fans of this identity. Notre Dame invokes Knute Rockne, the Gipper, and the Four Horsemen. USC hauls out the legendary Howard Jones, John McKay, Frank Gifford, Mike Garrett (we won't mention O.J.), and the other Heisman winners. What's the point of these rituals, repeated everywhere throughout the college football world? They are exercises in identity, in who we are. We are winners. We are big, tough, relentless, fleet of foot, defensive stone walls and offensive tidal waves. We never quit. We always prevail. What we have achieved *before* we will *again*.

I am not primarily a Johnson, a Smith, or a Jones. I am not primarily a minister, an electrician, or a shoemaker. I am not primarily an American, a Kenyan, or an Australian. I am not primarily a Californian, a Bavarian, or a Brazilian. I am not defined primarily by a given class, race, or social group. I'm not even my own person. I've been "bought with a price" (1 Corinthians 6:19–20). I've been crucified and I no longer live

(Galatians 2:20). I lost my life, having surrendered it to Christ (Matthew 16:24–25). My life now belongs to Jesus.

Taken on their own terms, there is nothing wrong with any of the above sources of identity. However, I must never allow a secondary identity to overtake the primary. If I do so, I make an idol of that identity and open the door to all manner of trouble. Who am I? It's simple. I am a Christian, a sinner saved by grace, a disciple of Christ.

Identity & Error

What happens when I allow my primary identity to become something other than that of disciple of Christ? What can I expect if I let something else, some secondary identity, to define who I am? This: I will become vulnerable to the idols, lusts, and losses that characterize that something else. We err, not just when we do that which is forbidden by God, but also when we pursue that which is permitted but do so in idolatrous proportions described above.

Let's return to the injured young athlete described previously. There is nothing inherently wrong with pursuing excellence in athletics. However, his identity "in Christ" was not firmly enough established. Consequently, when he lost his primary identity as a "Big Man on Campus" he was adrift amongst various alternative groups. Acceptance among the partiers required indulging drunkenness, illegal drugs, and promiscuity. "Partier" defined his identity, partying drove his behavior. As we saw, he fell, hook, line, and sinker.

What if I allow work to define me? Then success in that work will become my idol. Ambition to succeed, in proper proportion and balance is not evil. Hard work and excellence in one's vocation are virtues. However, they cease to be commendable when success is pursued above all else. Then the family may suffer. Church participation may suffer. Deprive me of success or recognition or promotion on the job and I may plunge into despair. Why? Because I have failed in that upon which my self-concept rests. My work is my identity. Ask me who I am and I answer, "I am an engineer at Aerospace, Inc." (or doctor, lawyer, businessman, ditch-digger, etc.). Deprive me of success and I may neglect other duties, or even do what is illegal, unfair, or dishonest to regain it. I may pursue recognition at all costs. If my identity is wrapped up in my reputation at work, then I am vulnerable to its excesses, its temptations, and its limitations.

What if I wrap up my identity in wealth? Then I am vulnerable to making an idol of the trappings of wealth. My image, my self-concept may be defined by things. I am that person who owns the luxury home, drives the luxury car, belongs to exclusive clubs, wears the finest clothes, goes on exotic vacations (which are promptly posted on Facebook for all to see). There is nothing evil in any of these things of themselves. Having and enjoying nice things is permitted. Yet if I allow them to control me, so that life is about image and comfort and pleasure, I will have made wealth an idol. A more superficial and pointless existence is hard to imagine.

What if I lose my wealth? Then I am psychologically shattered, devastated, angry, and lost, adrift, not knowing who I am and where I fit in. My place among the social elite is lost. I become vulnerable, as well, to the forms of "medication" that the depressed consume: drugs, alcohol, promiscuity, pornography, and so on.

What if my identity is wrapped up in something more obviously good, like family? What if my primary identity is as a father or mother, a husband or wife? Even then, I will have made that which is secondary primary. If the marriage is healthy and the children turn out fine, all is well in the world. What if they turn out bad? Or, what happens when the children grow up and leave? Many couples have identity crises. This is a well-known phenomenon. "Empty-nesters" become disoriented. Their whole life was their children. They literally say, "Now what?" Couples are known to divorce once their children leave because the foundation and purpose of their marriage was childrearing. They failed to understand their higher calling as disciples of Christ to glorify God.

A divorce can be particularly devastating when people have allowed themselves to be defined by their partners: "I am so-and-so's husband/wife." There is nothing wrong with this if it is a secondary identity. The problem arises, the vulnerability is manifested, when that family role is one's *primary* identity. The children leave, the spouse leaves, and one is not just devastated, but lost. One plunges into deep despair because one's whole identity is lost. I am a good mother/father/wife/husband. Now my family is gone. My marriage has broken up. What am I? Who am I?

Who am I? I am a servant of Christ, ready to serve in whatever capacity I am called. As we've seen, the Apostle Paul had much about which he could boast or draw security from in his world. He had an elite education, social and religious prestige, and political and legal status as a Roman citizen. Yet all that he regarded as "rubbish" as compared with the "surpassing worth" of knowing and serving Christ (Philippians 3:8). All the benefits, all the classifications, all the rewards of this world are secondary, indeed, a distant second to my identity as a disciple of Christ. That is who I am, and none of the losses and crosses of this life can affect that identity.

5. Mistaken Identity—1

Or do you not know that the unrighteous will not inherit the kingdom of God? Do not be deceived: neither the sexually immoral, nor idolaters, nor adulterers, nor men who practice homosexuality, nor thieves, nor the greedy, nor drunkards, nor revilers, nor swindlers will inherit the kingdom of God. And such were some of you. But you were washed, you were sanctified, you were justified in the name of the Lord Jesus Christ and by the Spirit of our God. (1 Corinthians 6:9–11)

Rosaria Champagne Butterfield provides a classic account of the destructive power of embracing a *false identity* in her autobiographical account of her conversion, *The Secret Thoughts of an Unlikely Convert*. It also reminds us of the importance of Christians having their identity rooted in their relationship to Christ.

At the age of 28 years, Rosaria was finishing a PhD in English Literature & Cultural Studies and working as a teaching associate in the Women's Studies Department at Syracuse University, one of the strongest such departments in the nation. Rosaria "came out," and "boldly declared myself lesbian," as she expressed it.[1] By the age of 36 she was a tenured associate professor at Syracuse in the English Department with teaching responsibilities in the Center for Women's Studies. She was in a lesbian relationship, was actively involved in a variety of causes, especially of the lesbian and gay variety. She sported a butch haircut and was a member of the Unitarian Universalist Church.

In 1997 she wrote an article criticizing the Promise Keepers movement. Ken Smith, a local Presbyterian minister (Reformed Presbyterian Church of North America or "Covenanters") wrote her a thoughtful response that was challenging, but not condemning. She called him. He and his wife Floy invited her for dinner. Awkward at first, nevertheless two years of off and on meetings with Ken and Floy followed, discussing Scripture and her heart. "I couldn't come to church," she said, "it would have been too threatening, too weird, too much."[2] She began to read the Bible "voraciously and compulsively," for about five hours a day.[3] Her graduate students, many of whom shared her opinions, found Ken dangerous, but she "thought he was safe in a dangerous way."[4] Finally, February 14, 1999, she "emerged from the bed of her lesbian lover and an hour later was sitting in a pew at the Syracuse Reformed Presbyterian Church."[5] Increasingly she realized that Jesus would brook no compromises. A university chaplain told her she could become a Christian and remain a lesbian. "This was a very appealing prospect," she admitted. However, she continues, "I had been reading and re-reading Scripture, and there are no such marks of postmodern 'both/and' in the Bible."[6]

Conversion

Her conversion she likens to an "alien abduction,"[7] a "train wreck,"[8] to "a complicated and comprehensive chaos,"[9] and to "the peace inside the eye of the hurricane."[10] Conversion for her was difficult because in her case, she says, "my feelings of lesbianism were familiar, comfortable, and recognizable, and I was reluctant to give them up."[11] When Christ claimed her for Himself, "the life that I had known and loved came to a humiliating end."[12] One night she prayed,

> and asked God if the gospel message was for someone like me, too. I viscerally felt the living presence of God as I prayed. Jesus seemed present and alive. I knew that I was not alone in my room. I prayed that if Jesus was truly a real and risen God, that he would change my heart. And if he was real and if I was his, I prayed that he would give me the strength of mind to follow him and the character to become a godly woman. I prayed for the strength of character to repent for a sin that at that time didn't feel like sin at all—it felt like life, plain and simple. I prayed that if my life was actually his life, that he would take it back and make it what he wanted it to be. I asked him to take it all: my sexuality, my profession, my community, my tastes, my books, and my tomorrows.[13]

Things quickly became very difficult for Rosaria. She was leaving a familiar world and entering a strange and forbidding one. Yet, she is thankful that,

> God sent me to a Reformed and Presbyterian conservative church to repent, heal, learn and thrive. The pastor there did not farm me out to a para-church ministry "specializing" in "gay people." ... I needed (and need) faithful shepherding, not the glitz and glamor that has captured the soul of modern evangelical culture. I had to lean and lean hard on the full weight of scripture, on the fullness of the word of God, and I'm grateful that when I heard the Lord's call on my life, *and I wanted to hedge my bets, keep my girlfriend and add a little God to my life, I had*

a pastor and friends in the Lord who asked nothing less of me than that I die to myself. Biblical orthodoxy can offer real compassion, because in our struggle against sin, we cannot undermine God's power to change lives.[14]

Identity

Key to Rosaria's conversion was understanding that being a lesbian *"was a case of mistaken identity."*[15] She became convinced that "homosexuality—like all sin—is symptomatic and not causal."[16] She acknowledges that her "lesbian identity began in non-sexual ways. I have always enjoyed the good communication that women share. I also found myself bonding with women over shared hobbies and interests and feminist and leftist political values."[17] Only gradually did her relations with other women take on an erotic dimension. Lesbian became what she was. It *defined* her. No longer was it merely a set of behaviors and opinions. It was her identity.

Consequently, conversion meant a new identity. Rosaria had to rethink who she was before God. She struggled to find her new Christian self-concept. First, she had to understand her identity as a Christian woman. Then she had to understand her identity as a married Christian woman, for eventually she married a man who would become a minister in the Reformed Presbyterian Church of North America. She explains,

Making a life commitment to Christ was not merely a philosophical shift. It was not a one-step process. It did not involve rearranging the surface prejudices and fickle loyalties of my life. Conversion didn't "fit" my life. Conversion overhauled my soul and personality. It was arduous and intense. I experienced with great depth the power and authority of God in my life. In it I learned—and am still learning—how to love God with all my heart, soul, strength and mind. When you die to yourself, you have nothing from your past to use as clay out of which to shape your future.[18]

Yet, the struggles remained. "The old patterns were there waiting for me, *and they knew my name.*"[19] Even as she writes she admits,

> It is dangerous to look back on my life, from the perspective of a lover and follower of Christ, now also a wife and a mother. It is painful to lay my hand on the absence of my former life, and breathe. My former life still lurks in the edges of my heart, shiny and still like a knife.[20]

Who is Rosaria Champagne Butterfield? She was, in a sense, never a lesbian. "And such *were* some of you," the Apostle Paul says of the sexually immoral, adulterers, homosexuals, drunkards, and the rest (1 Corinthians 6:9–11). She was engaged in lesbian behavior, embraced a lesbian worldview, and was immersed in the lesbian community. However, this should never have defined her. She was always a woman made by God and for God, whose purpose for her was to be found in creation, providence, and redemption. We can say that biology is destiny because God is the author of biology. The mind of God is revealed by the acts of God. His purpose is known in His design. She was and is a woman made for God, for marriage, for motherhood, for Christian discipleship, for Christian service, and for work in God's world.

In coming to Christ, Rosaria learned this lesson. Some people never do. Instead they fight their God-given design. They resist their identity as created and redeemed. When she finally married at the age of 39, she was shocked to realize that she was too old to have children. Her insights are profound.

I had spent my childbearing years fighting windmills and now I was, yet again, waking up to my life. There is a biblical principle that lies behind my confusion: people whose lives are riddled with unrestrained sin act like rebellious children. Sin, when unrestrained, infantilizes a person. Here I had thought that I was so mature, so capable, so "important" in the world, and the truth remains that I didn't even know how to act my age! After conversion, I was surprised to discover how old I really was.[21]

Who are we? Our identity is always to be defined by our relation to God, not our current or past behavior. We are children of God and servants of God. We are sinners and we are saints. We are sojourners and siblings. We are made in the image of God and find our satisfaction only in knowing God. We are disciples of Christ. Never are we to allow our idols, lusts, or false gods to define us. Our counsel to those struggling with sexual orientation, or for that matter, with alcohol, drugs, theft, gluttony, consumerism, pride or self-righteousness is this: don't ever let sin define who you are. I may have stolen. But I am not a thief. By grace, by adoption in Christ Jesus, I am a child of God. That is my true identity.

6. Mistaken Identity—2

I appeal to you, brothers, by the name of our Lord Jesus Christ, that all of you agree, and that there be no divisions among you, but that you be united in the same mind and the same judgment. For it has been reported to me by Chloe's people that there is quarreling among you, my brothers. What I mean is that each one of you says, "I follow Paul," or "I follow Apollos," or "I follow Cephas," or "I follow Christ." Is Christ divided? Was Paul crucified for you? Or were you baptized in the name of Paul? (1 Corinthians 1: 10–13)

Among the problems that the American of today faces is what political scientists call Balkanization and academics call identity studies. Americans are seeing themselves less as Americans, and more as hyphen-Americans, and often as aggrieved hyphen-Americans, Americans second, and minority identity first. Voting patterns reveal groups voting at rates approaching those of Soviet Republics, predictable at 80–90% on the basis of skin color, marital status, ethnic identity, or sexual preferences. Political philosophy, character, and accomplishments mean little when identity politics take over. What a given politician will do for my group means everything. All other considerations take a back seat. America, the America of the Declaration, the Constitution, and the Bill of Rights, the America of shared values and the common good, disappears. Group identity takes over, or rather, reasserts itself and the nation reverts to the ways of the Jim Crow South. Martin Luther King's vision of a color-blind America, Lady Justice with a blindfold, a land where one is judged by the content of one's character rather than the color of one's skin, is at risk.

Group Identity and the Church

What happens when identity politics seep into the church (which it seems the world's philosophies inevitably do)? Then theologians and clergymen begin to think increasingly in terms of race, ethnicity, and gender. No longer are we "mere catholics," as the Puritan Richard Baxter (1615–1691) would have us known; instead the conversation (and agitation) is about whether each group is properly represented, honored, and utilized. Objections begin to arise to the domination of "dead white males," and living ones, in the life of the church.

The positive context in which this discussion in the Church is occurring is the rapid expansion of Christianity in the non-western world. Extraordinary growth of the church has occurred in Africa, in Asia, and among Protestants in Latin America. This is a cause of rejoicing. It is anticipated that gifted leaders will emerge from the churches in these regions as indeed, they already have. Their books articles, sermons, lectures, music, and lyrics will be a great blessing to the wider Church. This should occur naturally and organically as excellence is recognized over time.

What should be resisted is on the one hand labeling the church as "western," or "European," and on the other hand introducing quotas into the church. What should be resisted is elevating leaders because of ethnicity, promoting literature in order to achieve racial or gender balance in reading lists, or introducing demographically specific music and lyrics into the regular worship of the church. Let me explain.

Identity and core beliefs

First, why should Christians care about the gender, ethnicity, race, or age of the source of its thoughts and practices? Why would the church want to evaluate its practices on the basis of skin color? or gender? or class? These are worldly categories that we are meant to transcend in Christ. Is it not the case that in the church we are neither Jew nor Greek, male nor female (Galatians 3:28)? Is it not our motto (borrowed by our American founding fathers), "out of the many, one?" We are "one new man" in Christ, *transcending* our worldly differences while not obliterating them (Ephesians 2:11ff). We no longer evaluate each other based on worldly categories (see James 2:1ff). We are to "know" or "regard" (ESV) no one "after the flesh" (2 Corinthians 5:16). If, for example, eighteenth century Germans and nineteenth century British were particularly gifted at musical composition, why should we hesitate to recognize this? Why fail fully to utilize their contributions though other ethnic groups may be "under-represented" according to the quota–obsessed? As to the source of the church's beliefs and practices, as long as they are godly and gifted sources, who cares?

Catholic or Western

Second, does this classifying of the church as "western" stand up to scrutiny? It certainly doesn't in terms of the church's theology and practices. Did the Scottish Presbyterians invent psalm-singing, or did the ancient monks of the Egypt desert? Was expository preaching an innovation of Calvin, or did he find it in the ancient church fathers Origen (*c.*185–254), considered the "father of biblical exposition," and Chrysostom (*c.*347–407), whose "plain style" expositions profoundly influenced Calvin, among others? Did the English Puritans invent extemporaneous prayer, or did they find it in Justin Martyr's *Apology*, dating about AD 155? As for church songs, take the *Trinity* hymnal I am most familiar with. It includes lyrics contributed to Clement of Alexandria (*c.*150–220), an Athenian but also a longtime resident of Egypt; Gregory of Nazianzus, of Cappadocia (see below); Prudentius (348–413), a Spaniard; John of Damascus (*c.*655–*c.*750), a Syrian; Andrew of Crete (*c.*660–740), a Syrian; and Joseph the Hymnographer (*c.*810–886), a Sicilian. Some contributions are very old and from unknown sources. The *Gloria Patri* dates to the second century, the *Gloria in Excelsis* to the fourth century, the *Te Deum* also the fourth century, the *Liturgy of St. James* (from which "Let All Mortal Flesh Keep Silence" was derived) from the fifth century, and so on. Musical contributions may be found from Hebrew, European, American, Hispanic, African, and African-American folk traditions. What exactly do we mean by western?

Here's the real surprise. Who were the prime movers in formulating the orthodox doctrines of the church, the theology of Nicea and Chalcedon? Who hammered out the doctrines of the Trinity and the dual nature of Christ? Surely they were westerners, Greeks or Romans, infected with the rationalism and logic so foreign to the non-western world, right? Wrong. As Thomas C. Oden has shown in his work, *How Africa Shaped the Christian Mind*, the flow of intellectual life in the first three centuries of the church was not north to south, but south to north. It flowed from Africa and the Middle East north to Europe.[1]

We can name two theologians to make our point: Athanasius

(of *contra mundum* fame) and Augustine (c.354–430), the former having decisive influence in defending the doctrine of the Trinity and the latter the most important theological mind in the history of the church. Athanasius (*c.*296–298–373), nicknamed the "black dwarf," was an Egyptian. So were Origen (*c.*185–*c.*254) and Cyril (*c.*315–87). Augustine (*c.*185–*c.*254) was a North African, as were Tertullian (*c.*160–*c.*225), known as the "Father of Latin Theology," Lactantius (*c.*240–*c.*320) and Cyprian (*c.*258).

The Cappadocian Fathers (Basil the Great [*c.*330–79], Gregory of Nyssa [*c.*330–*c.*395], and Gregory of Nazianzus [325–390]), of crucial influence in defeating Arianism, were all by birth from Caesarea in Cappadocia, that is, present day south-central Turkey.

The church was dominated by "non-western" leaders in the crucial formative years between the resurrection of Christ and the fall of Rome. We might also remember that Jesus and the Apostles were not westerners either. *We can only speak of the church as "western" in a highly qualified sense.* The Church's historic doctrines and practices are more rightly understood as catholic and Christian, not western.

Christian or European

Third, are the more obviously "western" elements of the church a product of the culture of the west or of the culture of the church? When Boniface (*c.*675–754), the "Apostle of Germany," and Ansgar (801–65), the "Apostle of the North" (Scandinavia), and Willibrord (658–739), the "Apostle of Frisia" (the Netherlands) evangelized their respective mission fields, did they find their hosts playing Bach fugues on their harpsichords and decorating their homes with Rembrandt's paintings?

The barbarian Europeans, pre-Christian, had no music to speak of and primitive art at best. Western music, with its harmony, melody, and rhythm, is, in an important sense, Christian music. It is the music that the Christian church developed, beginning with Gregorian chants and increasing in sophistication over the centuries. In our view, the church's location in the "west" is incidental. The ethnicity of its members is incidental. For most of the last 1400 years (since the Muslim conquests in the Middle East and North Africa), the church has been located primarily in Europe. The barbarian European converts took the musical heritage that the Patristic church handed to it and developed it, adding little from its distinctive barbarian culture, as the church shaped Europe, rather than Europe's barbarians shaping the church. It is ridiculous to think that pagan European converts demanded the inclusion of their primitive drums and dances in their church's services, so that the "style" of the service would be familiar to them. Instead the Christian church developed its own music, and Europe adopted what the church created. Indeed, we can even say the church created Europe. Europe is not a continent but merely the tip of the Eurasian land mass. "Europe" is a cultural phenomena distinguished historically from Asia primarily by its Christian civilization. It is an exceedingly difficult task to disentangle what is European from what is Christian.

Conclusion

The church has its own distinctive culture of liturgy, creeds, classical writings, music, devotional lyrics, and so on. It is painful to see "interest" groups vying for *their* style preferences in the church's worship: the young demanding pop music, ethnic groups *their* music, cowboys and hip-hoppers *their* music at *their* churches. Because I am a Christian, not a hyphenated Christian, I gratefully receive *the* Tradition, consisting of the church's Creeds, classic writings, music, devotional lyrics, and so on. I embrace the "catholic" hymnal, words and tunes. I refuse to join the Balkanizers who classify contributions to the Tradition according to their racial, ethnic, gender, and generational identities. I care only about excellence. Because we are "in Christ," we appreciate the contributions of the brethren according to their edifying capacities, whatever their worldly "identity," and judge them not "according to the flesh" (2 Corinthians 5:16).

I anticipate new additions to the catholic canon of excellent writings, music, and lyrics in the years ahead from non-western sources as the church continues its expansion into non-western regions.[2] What is our identity? Whatever our ethnicity, race, age, or gender, we are mere Christians.

*   *   *   *   *

We will now begin our positive exposition of Christian identity, distinguishing our *core* or *fundamental* identity (Sons [and Siblings], Sinners, Sheep, and Saints), from our *active* identity (Servants, Subjects, and Students), from our *contrary* or *contrasting* or even *combative* identity (Sojourners, Sportsmen, and Soldiers). These eleven elements are the various components in a healthy understanding of who we are in Christ.

III. Our Christian Identity

7. Our Core Identity:

Sons (and Siblings), Sinners, Saints, Sheep

... for in Christ Jesus you are all sons of God, through faith. For as many of you as were baptized into Christ have put on Christ. There is neither Jew nor Greek, there is neither slave nor free, there is no male and female, for you are all one in Christ Jesus. And if you are Christ's, then you are Abraham's offspring, heirs according to promise.
(Galatians 3:26–29)

My primary identity is that I am a Christian. This defines me over and above all transient sources of identity such as family, employment, race, class, or nationality. A Jew doesn't have to cease being a Jew in coming to Christ, and a Gentile doesn't have to cease being a Gentile in coming to Christ, or a man a man or a woman a woman. Worldly classifications are secondary—it matters not in God's kingdom if I am Jew or Greek, slave or free, male or female. We "are all one," the same, "*in Christ.*" This identity shapes my response to circumstances, overcoming all secondary identities. I respond first as a Christian. Subsequently and only in light of that Christian identity do I respond in ways suited to my family, vocation, ethnicity, and so on.

A 55-year-old, highly successful self-employed lawyer gives his daughter in marriage, his last of five children to wed. Within six months he contracts an aggressive form of cancer. Surgery and treatments force him to take a leave of absence. Always physically fit, his body deteriorates. His wife, distressed by her new empty nest, can't cope with the additional stress of his condition, and legally separates from him. His whole external identity is shattered in a matter of months. Income plunges. Bills pile up. He is a shadow of his former self. Everything that defined him is gone: his profession, his success, his affluence, his role as husband and father, his health. Where does this leave him?

Secure. As a Christian he is safe. Great sadness has entered his life. Of course he is grieved. Yet nothing fundamental has changed. Shifting external circumstances leave the eternal verities untouched. His core identity is unchanged. Who he is remains the same. How so?

Sonship

He is still a child of God. God is not our Father by birth but by rebirth. By nature we are excluded from the family of God and the privileges of family membership. It is only to those who "receive Him," Jesus, "who believe in His name," that He gives "the right to become children of God" (John 1:12). God's children are those "who were born, not of blood nor of the will of the flesh nor of the will of man, but of God" (John 1:13).

Our shattered lawyer received the "adoption as sons" the moment he believed (Galatians 4:5). His sins were forgiven. He was reconciled to God. He was given the gift of eternal life. He was saved. Nothing can *undo* that. Nothing can *threaten* that.

Knowing that I am a child of God shapes the way that we

look at, well, almost everything. *Prayer.* How do I pray? As a child to our Father. Jesus teaches us to pray, "Our Father" (Matthew 6:9). Jesus asks us:

> Or which one of you, if his son asks him for bread, will give him a stone? Or if he asks for a fish, will give him a serpent? If you then, who are evil, know how to give good gifts to your children, how much more will your Father who is in heaven give good things to those who ask him! (Matthew 7:9–11)

Whenever we pray, we call upon an Almighty God who is our Father, and consequently always hears us with interest and sympathy, whatever our earthly adversities might bring. He never ceases to pity me as a father pities his children (Psalm 103:13).

Why do we *obey* and *serve* God? Jesus teaches us it is to please our Father. We "practice righteousness" not to be seen by others, but in secret, for the secret rewards of our Father (Matthew 6:1–8; 16–18). "We are under obligation," says the Apostle Paul in discussion of the spirit of adoption and our responsibility to love not according to the flesh but according to the Spirit (Romans 8:12ff). Sonship underscores rather than undermines our duty to please, to obey and to serve. William Gurnall (1617–1679) in his classic, *The Christian in Complete Armour*, calls pleasing God "the highest project and ultimate end" of the believer.[1] The Apostle Paul says "we make our own" our "ambition" (NASB) "to please him" (2 Corinthians 5:9). We are charged to "be imitators of God, *as beloved children*" and to "walk in love, as Christ loved us" (Ephesians 5:1–2).

How am I to understand *adversity*? Nothing happens by chance. Never am I a victim of "bad luck." I know that all that I endure comes to me by the hand of my loving Father who "disciplines (us) for our good that we may share in His holiness" and "bear the peaceful fruit of righteousness" (Hebrews 12:5–13). God's children have an eternal perspective. We are able to forgo the "passing pleasures of sin" because we have in view a heavenly reward (Hebrews 11:25–26). Suffering now is made bearable by the confidence that a rich family inheritance awaits us as children of God. Even in this world, two people working in miserable conditions would differ in their attitudes if both labored for a dollar an hour all year long but one was promised a ten million dollar reward at the end of the year and the other was not. The promise of family inheritance then transforms our outlook now. So the Apostle Paul says next

> For I consider that the sufferings of this present time are not worth comparing with the glory that is to be revealed to us. (Romans 8:18)

How can we have *assurance*? Because we are safe in the Father's hands (John 10:29), we are absolutely secure. No one can pry open the protective grip of omnipotence. We cry "Abba, Father," knowing that nothing can separate us from the love of God which is ours in Christ Jesus (Galatians 4:6; Romans 8:15–17, 31–39). Sonship is the key to our hope of heaven. The Holy Spirit is "the Spirit of adoption" (Romans 8:15). The Spirit bears witness that we are children of God, "and if children," says the Apostle, "then heirs."

> And if children, heirs also, heirs of God and fellow heirs with Christ, if indeed we suffer with Him so that we may also be glorified with Him. (Romans 8:17)

How are we to live a *life of faith*? We are able to do so in the confidence that God is our Father. Jesus urges us not to be anxious for life, for what we will eat, drink, and clothe ourselves. Listen as He questions us and reveals the solution:

> Look at the birds of the air: they neither sow nor reap nor gather into barns, and yet your heavenly Father feeds them. Are you not of more value than they? (Matthew 6:26)

Our Father feeds the birds and He considers us, his children, as far more valuable than they. "Therefore do not be anxious," He tells us, about what we will eat, drink and wear, for "your heavenly Father knows that you need them all" (Matthew 6:31–32). We can seek first the kingdom of God and not be anxious about life's basic provisions because God is our Father and will take care of us.

How are we to view time and eternity? Sonship is also key to our hope of heaven. The Spirit bears witness that we are children of God, "and if children," says the Apostle, "then heirs."

> and if children, heirs also, heirs of God and fellow heirs with Christ, if indeed we suffer with Him so that we may also be glorified with Him. (Romans 8:17)

God's children have an eternal perspective. We are able to forgo the "passing pleasures of sin" because we have in view a heavenly reward (Hebrews 11:25–26). Suffering now is made bearable by the confidence that a rich heavenly inheritance awaits us. Even in this world two people working in miserable conditions would differ in their attitudes if both labored for a dollar an hour all year long, but one was promised a ten million dollar bonus at the end of the year and the other wasn't. So the Apostle Paul says

> For I consider that the sufferings of this present time are not worth comparing with the glory that is to be revealed to us. (Romans 8:18)

Because we are sons, we are heirs and co-heirs of all that there is. One is tempted to say that *everything* about the Christian life revolves around the concept of sonship. Because we have received "the grace of adoption," says the *Westminster Confession of Faith*, we "enjoy the liberties and privileges of the children of God," we "have access to the throne of grace with boldness," and "are pitied, protected, provided for, and chastened by him, as by a father, and yet never cast off, but sealed to the day of redemption" (XII.1).

Siblings

Because we are sons, we are also siblings. We are not alone, we are not solitary. Sibling is not a biblical word, "brethren" is the term the Bible uses. But bear with me: for sake of mnemonic harmony I need an "S" word, so it's "siblings."

This second component of Christian identity is membership in the body of Christ and it is actually an aspect of sonship. As we've seen, all believers are children of God the Father. This makes us brothers and sisters. Believers are called "brethren" (*adelphotēs*), or "brothers," 47 times in Acts, 92 times in the epistles. Female believers are referred to as "sisters" (*adelphē*) another six times, for a total of 145 "family" references, making this the dominant way the New Testament refers to believers. We are brethren with an elder Brother and common Father (Romans 8:29; 8:14–17). Our siblings may be very different from us. They may be another race or class or culture but nevertheless we are family (Galatians 3:29). We are members of God's "household" (Ephesians 2:19). Who am I? I am a part of the body of Christ. I am a citizen of God's kingdom. I am a member of the church of Christ. I am a child in the family of God.

People often wrap up their identity in their associations. They are members of a given club, a given team, a given profession, a given nationality or locality. Associations *define* many people. Gauging from the decals, flags, and stickers on pick-up trucks all over the region I live in, some people are proud of their connection to the University of Georgia. They are Georgia fans. Above all else, *they are Dawgs* (that is, dogs, as in bulldogs, the Georgia mascot, pronounced with a southern accent). Without necessarily ceasing to be any of those things that we are through our associations, the Christian's primary association is that of membership in the church of Christ. I am that before I am anything else with which I am associated.

The church then, because it is the church *of Christ*, is my first commitment and my first loyalty. Its health, its well-being, its effectiveness, its fruitfulness, are my first priority. We can speak, in a carefully nuanced way, of the church coming before the family (see Luke 14:26). Certainly I am never to let the work of the church become an excuse to neglect my familial duties. However, neither am I to allow the family to preempt my commitment to the body of Christ. Why? Because the church is my new family. Jesus is the first-born among many brethren (Romans 8:29). We are siblings. We are children of God by faith, and as such "fellow-heirs with Christ" (Romans 8:14–17). Because we are sons of God and heirs, our worldly associations and identities recede into the background. Our secondary identities as Jews or Greeks, slaves or free, male or female, *are all superseded by our primary identity as members of God's family* (Galatians 3:26–4:7). We are now "of God's household" (Ephesians 2:19), calling upon one Father (Ephesians 4:6). This family identity has important implications. Because this component of Christian identity is often overlooked, we will develop it further.

Responsible

The first implication of belonging to the household of God is that we are responsible for each other. I've heard it said, "The family is that place where when you can come home they have to take you." There is considerable truth in this. So also in the family of God. We are responsible for each other. We look out for each other. We are to be "devoted to one another in brotherly love," along with a whole list of things (Romans 12:10–21; see also 1 Corinthians 12). We have "communion in each other's gifts and graces" and are "obligated" to promote the "mutual good" of all the saints, says the *Westminster Confession of Faith* (XXVI.1). By my count there are 28 different "one anothers" in the New Testament, detailing all that we are to do for each other, including pray for each other (James 5:16). Really there is only one: love one another, repeated 13 times (e.g. John 13:34; 15:12, 17; Romans 13:8, etc.). I am my brother's keeper. "O Christians!" says Gurnall. "You were conceived in the same womb of the church, begotten by the same seed of the word to this new creation."[2] You are of one blood and one family. How can you not love one another?

Accountable

We are also accountable to each other. Why else would we be commanded to *confess our sins* to one another (James 5:16), or *admonish* one another (Colossians 3:16), or *submit* to one another (Ephesians 5:21), or *exhort* one another (Hebrews 3:13)? Who would dare to exhort another? Those who *would* dare might be labeled busy-bodies and invite a punch in the nose. Yet we are accountable to one another:

> Brothers, if anyone is caught in any transgression, you who are

spiritual should restore him in a spirit of gentleness. Keep watch on yourself, lest you too be tempted. (Galatians 6:1)

"Brothers," he says, i.e. brothers, sisters, *siblings*, you are accountable to each other. We can become alienated from the family through sin, and be restored through the actions of those who are spiritual. No longer may we live in whatever way that we may wish to live. We are accountable.

Again:

But now I am writing to you not to associate with anyone who bears the name of brother if he is guilty of sexual immorality or greed, or is an idolater, reviler, drunkard, or swindler—not even to eat with such a one ... God judges those outside. "Purge the evil person from among you." (1 Corinthians 5:11, 13)

The Apostle Paul deals specifically with one who is a "brother." Our behavior is the business of us all; we are accountable to each other. Bad behavior is to be identified and shunned, even as far as not to "eat with such a one." My sin is the business of my Christian "brother" (sibling!). If I am indulging some sin my Christian sibling is to "reprove" me. If the erring sibling doesn't listen, we take witnesses. If he still doesn't listen, *tell it to the church. And if he refuses to listen even to the church, let him be to you as a Gentile and a tax collector* (Matthew 18:17).

Reliable

We are both *responsible* and *accountable* because we are meant to be able to *rely* on each other. You are meant to look out for me and I am meant to look out for you. We are meant to *be there* for each other, bearing one another's burdens (Galatians 6:2). This is why we take vows. Far too often people join the church as though they were joining a health club. They go when it suits their needs. If another health club opens that is more convenient, or better meets their needs as they perceive them, they go there. When church membership is treated in this way, a trail of broken relationships is left behind.

The church is a family by covenant. The church, going back to Abraham, has always been a family by covenant, entered into by covenant signs (circumcision and baptism) and regularly reaffirmed by covenant meals (Passover and the Lord's Supper; see Genesis 17:11; Romans 4:11; Colossians 2:11). Membership, like marriage vows, make the commitment to God and each other explicit, and permanent. We are meant to be able to count on each other.

Ownership

We can use another extra-biblical term to summarize what we mean by responsible and accountable family membership. We are all to take *ownership* of the church. The church is *my* family, it is *my* church, in the best sense of that pronoun. Its members are my brothers and sisters. This means that I can be both an *advocate* and an *apologist* for the church. Outside the church and within it I am to positively affirm and explain what we do and why we do it, and why it is good that we do things as we do them. When attacked, I am an apologist, *defending* the church's life and ministry. I eagerly labor to advance the health, the well-being, and the fruitfulness of the church and its mission.

I am to *love* the church. Of course I am to love Christ, but I am to love His church as well. Jesus loves His bride: He nourishes and cherishes it, He shed His blood on its behalf (Ephesians 5:22ff). He is building His church (Matthew 16:18).

So I am to love my Christian siblings individually and in their collective identity as the church, the family of God.

Rodney Stark, in his books *The Rise of Christianity* and *The Triumph of Christianity*, has reminded us of the importance of the quality of the Christian community's "life together." He reviews church history from the perspective of a sociologist. The growth of the Christian church, its conquest of the Roman Empire, he maintains, has everything to do with the mutual care of the early Christians. "O how they love one another," Tertullian reports even pagans exclaimed. When devastating plagues struck the Roman Empire in the 2nd and again in the 3rd centuries, pagans abandoned the sick and Christians cared for them. They cared for the widows and orphans. They cared for the poor and needy. When coupled with high moral standards, the church becomes a city set upon a hill, a light shining in the darkness drawing the unbelieving world into its embrace (Matthew 5:14–16).

Sinners

Our reeling lawyer is also a sinner. Yes, he is a son and a sibling. He also is a saint, as we will see. Yet his suffering at the hands of others leaves no room for self-righteousness.

While sin may no longer define us, the Apostles are careful to remind us of its continuing presence. The Apostles never lost sight of the fact that by nature we are sinners. Our old sinful self was crucified with Christ (Romans 6:6). We are new creations in Christ (2 Corinthians 5:17). Yet the remnants of the "old self" remains and must continually be "put off" (Ephesians 4:22; Colossians 3:9). Our identity as children of God does not cancel our identity as sinners. "Whilst blood is in my veins," says George Swinnock in his classic work, *The Christian Man's*

Calling, "sin will be in my soul."[3] We are redeemed sinners, saved sinners, transformed sinners, yet sinners nonetheless. The Apostle Paul retains a low opinion of himself. As far as he is concerned, he is the "chief of sinners" (1 Timothy 1:15, KJV). He is a "nobody" (2 Corinthians 12:11). He is the "least of the apostles and not fit to be called an apostle" (1 Corinthians 15:9). "O how he batters his pride, and speaks himself all the naught," says Gurnall. "No enemy could have drawn his picture with blacker coal."[4] He is even "the very least of all the saints" (Ephesians 3:8). The Apostle Paul—who is not adverse to employing irony—seems to describe himself in these ways without any irony at all. Add to these self-effacing self-descriptions the monumental struggle of Romans 7:14ff and the sober recognition that "nothing good dwells in me" (Romans 7:18), and we have an important element of the Christian self-concept. "Wretched man that I am," the Apostle cries (Romans 7:24). The Apostles retained a realistic estimate of the capacities of the redeemed soul and of the darker propensities of our nature.

This aspect of our identity has not always been appreciated. Sometimes is has been disparagingly referred to as "worm theology." Victims of this emphasis on our sinfulness have been portrayed as "wallowing in guilt," living a gloomy and joyless life. Over the years various movements have sprung up assuring believers that they could experience a "victorious" life, live the "higher life," or enjoy "abundant life." The "Keswick" Movement urged believers to "let go and let God" so that they might be liberated from the terrible burden of "striving" against "besetting" sin. More recent concerns have been expressed regarding the input of worm theology on "self-image" and "self-esteem."

Yet Jesus commends "those who mourn" for their sin, for

they and they alone "shall be comforted." He commends not self-regard but poverty of spirit (Matthew 5:3–4). B. B. Warfield (1851–1921) wrote that the "'miserable-sinner' conception of the Christian life has moulded the piety of all the Protestant generations." Even as believers we are still "wrath-deserving sinners," though regarded as saints, forgiven, and credited with the righteousness of Christ.[5] "Often meditate on thy own personal miscarriages," Gurnall urges.[6] Ralph Venning's *The Sinfulness of Sin* provides an example of how classic Protestantism found benefit in contemplating the evil of sin: its nature, its causes, its properties, its effects, and so on.[7] "We should endeavor to get our hearts broken for sin, ashamed of sin, and fired with indignation against sin," says Swinnock.[8] There is a proper "worm" theology that serves as a catalyst for thanksgiving. "Alas and did my Savior bleed and did my sovereign die? Would he devote that sacred head for such a *worm* as I?"[9] Are we to wallow in guilt? No, we are to wallow in grace. The deeper our understanding of the black backdrop of personal sin and guilt the more the diamond of grace sparkles. It leads to deeper insight into God's "amazing pity, grace unknown, and love beyond degree."[10] The greater the clarity with which one recognizes personal depravity the greater appears the love of Christ for sinners. The one who is forgiven much loves much (Luke 7:47).

Luther's formula helps us: we are *simul jus et peccator*, at once justified and sinner. We are declared righteous by the judicial verdict of God because of our faith in the Christ of the cross. Yet we continue to remind ourselves of the evil of sin, of our fallen nature, of our old self who is still dangerously active (Ephesians 4:22ff; Colossians 3:5–11). Why? To keep us humble, vigilant and dependent.

Only as we meditate can the sinfulness of sin and our own

vulnerability to its enticements will we recognize and abhor its presence. Swinnock asks the questions he would have us all ask:

> What sorrow for it (sin) can be sufficient! What hatred of it can be enough! What watchfulness against it, what self-abhorrency, because I have loved it, and lived in it, can equal its desert! Oh that I could weep bitterly for the commission of it, and watch narrowly for the prevention of it, and pray fervently for pardon of it and power against it![11]

"Be killing sin or sin will be killing you," John Owen (1616–1683) warns.[12] Reminding ourselves of our continuing depravity is a hedge against arrogance, carelessness, and over-confidence. Only when we are conscious of our weakness do we depend on God's power rather than our own strength. God's power is perfected in weakness. Only when we know we are weak are we truly strong (2 Corinthians 12:9). Even our trials in life are divinely designed to teach us to "rely not on ourselves" (2 Corinthians 1:9). When we behave in the world "with sympathy and godly simplicity" we are able to do so not because we possess "earthly wisdom" but only "by the grace of God" (2 Corinthians 1:12). A "pure and blameless" life, one "filled with the fruit of righteousness […] *comes through Jesus Christ*" (Philippians 1:11). Soul bracing realism about our vulnerability to and propensity for evil is necessary if we are to depend on the True Vine apart from whom "we can do nothing" (John 15:1–5).

Saints

At the same time, we are saints. Sixty-one times in the New Testament believers are called *hagioi*, saints, meaning "holy ones." By way of comparison, believers are called "Christians" (*christianos*) but three times, and only once are they so labeled in a positive sense (1 Peter 4:16).[13] We are sinners, and, however counter-intuitive it may seem, we are also saints. Typically Paul opens his epistles by addressing "all the saints" in a given location (e.g. 2 Corinthians 1:1; Ephesians 1:1; Philippians 1:1; Colossians 1:2; Philemon 5; cf. Romans 1:7; 16:5; 1 Corinthians 1:2; Hebrews 13:2–4). Saints are not dead clergymen, as the old joke goes. They're not even especially committed Christians, as when we say, "She's a saint." Saints, holy ones, are ordinary Christians, which raises a question: how can the sinners we've just described above be called "holy"? I certainly don't think of myself as "holy." I'm far more comfortable with the label "chief of sinners" than "saint."

Still, there are two important senses in which we can rightly conceive of ourselves as holy. The first is the *judicial* sense we've just mentioned. God has rendered a verdict respecting us. We are saints because God looks at us in Christ and sees not only pardoned sins but imputed righteousness. That is, He sees us credited or clothed with the righteousness of Christ. When He contemplates us, He sees Christ and His perfections (Romans 4:1–13; 5:12–21). Our holiness, then, is a *status* conferred rather than a description of character or behavior. It has sometimes been called a *positional* truth rather than a *descriptive* one. Yet what a truth it is! On the basis of our imputed righteousness/ holiness the Apostle Paul can speak of our justification and glorification in the past tense (the Greek perfect), as a completed action (Romans 8:30). So certain is our heavenly destiny that he can speak of us as already glorified. Indeed, we have already been "seated with (Christ) in the heavenly places" (Ephesians 2:6). Salvation can be no more safe or secure than that.

The second sense in which we can be spoken of as "saints" is in the *practical s*ense of our sanctification. We have become holy in practice. The Apostles often look back at the believer's non-Christian past, yet always they do so to identify what they once were but are no more. The Apostle Paul lists the sexually immoral, idolaters, adulterers, homosexuals and others among the Corinthian believers only to say, "And such were some of you."

> Or do you not know that the unrighteous will not inherit the kingdom of God? Do not be deceived: neither the sexually immoral, nor idolaters, nor adulterers, nor men who practice homosexuality, nor thieves, nor the greedy, nor drunkards, nor revilers, nor swindlers will inherit the kingdom of God. And such were some of you. But you were washed, you were sanctified, you were justified in the name of the Lord Jesus Christ and by the Spirit of our God. (1 Corinthians 6:9–11)

That is what you *were*. You *were* idolaters. You *were* adulterers. You *were* thieves. You *were* drunkards. That sinful identity no longer defines you. "You were washed, you were sanctified, you were justified in the name of the Lord Jesus Christ and by the Spirit of our God."

"Remember," he tells the Ephesian Gentiles in the flesh, "you were at that time separated from Christ, alienated from the commonwealth of Israel and strangers to the covenants of promise, having no hope and without God in the world" (Ephesians 2:12). That's what you once were, but you are no more:

> But now in Christ Jesus you who once were far off have been brought near by the blood of Christ. (Ephesians 2:13).

"But now" you are not what you "once were." Then you were "far off," but now you "have been brought near." A second time the Apostle reminds his Ephesian readers of the world out of which they have come:

> Now this I say and testify in the Lord, that you must no longer walk as the Gentiles do, in the futility of their minds. They are darkened in their understanding, alienated from the life of God because of the ignorance that is in them, due to their hardness of heart. They have become callous and have given themselves up to sensuality, greedy to practice every kind of impurity. (Ephesians 4:17–19)

What were you? You were "darkened [...] alienated [...] callous [...] given (up) to sensuality [...] greedy [...] practice(ing) every level of impurity." Then comes another of the Apostle's wonderful transitional words: "But" (cf 2:4, 13). That is what they are, that is what they do. "But that is not" what you are:

> But that is not the way you learned Christ!—assuming that you have heard about him and were taught in him, as the truth is in Jesus, to put off your old self, which belongs to your former manner of life and is corrupt through deceitful desires, and to be renewed in the spirit of your minds, and to put on the new self, created after the likeness of God in true righteousness and holiness. (Ephesians 4:20–24)

The "truth" that you were taught "in Jesus" is that the "old self," the old person that you were is to be "put off," disposed of, and the "new self" that you have become "put on." That new self is defined by "true righteousness and holiness." That is your new identity.

We have the same in the Apostle's instructions to Titus:

> For we ourselves were once foolish, disobedient, led astray,

slaves to various passions and pleasures, passing our days in malice and envy, hated by others and hating one another. (Titus 3:3)

Here is what "we ourselves were once." Then he lists: "foolish, disobedient, led astray, slaves to various passions" and so on. Yet what we were we are no longer:

But when the goodness and loving kindness of God our Savior appeared, he saved us, not because of works done by us in righteousness, but according to his own mercy, by the washing of regeneration and renewal of the Holy Spirit, whom he poured out on us richly through Jesus Christ our Savior. (Titus 3:4–6)

There it is again: "But when." A decisive, defining change has occurred. A line can be drawn across the life of the believer. There is a before and an after. Each person of the Trinity is identified in this great work of rescue. When once "God (the Father) our Savior appeared," and Jesus Christ our Savior "poured out on us richly" the Holy Spirit, and the Spirit washed us through "regeneration and renewal," everything changed. What we were, we are no more. We have a new identity.

Similarly, the Apostle Peter urges his readers in 1 Peter 4:1–5 to "arm (them)selves" with right thinking that they might "cease from sin,"

so as to live for the rest of the time in the flesh no longer for human passions but for the will of God. (1 Peter 4:2)

"No longer" they are to live the way they once did "for human passions." For "the rest of the time" that they have to live, they are to live "for the will of God."

For the time that is past suffices for doing what the Gentiles want to do, living in sensuality, passions, drunkenness, orgies, drinking parties, and lawless idolatry. (1 Peter 4:3)

The emphasis again is that these corrupt practices of the pagans, of the Gentiles, are in the past. "The time that is past suffices" for doing what is characteristic of pagans. This is what you did in your previous life. That is who you were. Enough is enough. You are now part of a different world:

> With respect to this they are surprised when you do not join them in the same flood of debauchery, and they malign you; but they will give account to him who is ready to judge the living and the dead. (1 Peter 4:4–5)

The Apostle divides the world into us and them. "You do not join them" in their flood of "debauchery," and they "malign you" as a result. Your restraint is incomprehensible to them. You are not a part of their world anymore and as a result, they are both puzzled and angered.

That unbelieving world and the believers' past involvement in that world is over. It is antithetical to what believers now are. It is impossible that the past would continue in any way to form part of their identity, as though a believer might be known as "James the drunk" or "Thomas the adulterer" or "Peter the idolater." We may not be known as "gay Christians" or "porn Christians" or "same-sex attracted" or "other spouse attracted."[14] As Rosaria Butterfield has said, "We are not our sin, and we ought never to let it define us."[15]

The enslaving power of sin has been broken in Christ. Our old selves were buried with Christ and raised up in newness of life (Romans 6:1–8). Sin can no longer be master over us (Romans 6:8). We are new creations in Christ Jesus. The old ways, the old loves, the old habits, the old controlling appetites have "passed away" and all things have "become new" (2 Corinthians 5:17). God has made the spiritually dead "alive together with Christ" (Ephesians 2:5).

This means that real growth in holiness takes place in the redeemed. We are *becoming* holy. We are *increasingly* holy. We are putting off the old ways and putting on the new virtues (Ephesians 4:17ff; Colossians 3:1ff). We are putting sin to death (Romans 8:13; Colossians 3:5), crucifying the flesh and its lusts (Galatians 5:24; 6:14). We are dying to sin and living to righteousness (1 Peter 2:24). We are increasingly manifesting the fruit of the Spirit (Galatians 5:22ff). We are increasingly growing in Christ-likeness, following in His steps, imitating His virtues, and reproducing His love (1 Peter 2:21; Philippians 2:5ff; 1 John 4:7–11).

So expected is this growth in holiness, so certain, so inevitable, that the Apostles not only rejoice in its certainty, but also warn of its absence. There is a practical holiness without which no one will see the Lord (Hebrews 12:14). Christ not only liberates us from the *penalty* of sin but its *power*. He not only *justifies* us but also *sanctifies* us. He not only releases us of *guilt* but cleanses us from *corruption*. He not only *imputes* righteousness but *imparts* it. The liberty that Christ brings is comprehensive.

Sheep

Another important element of our core identity that highlights our weakness is that of sheep. It is an ancient metaphor by which God has taught His people about Himself and about themselves. He is the Shepherd (Psalm 23:1; 78:52; 80:1). We are His sheep (Psalm 74:1; 79:13; 95:7; 100:3).

Shepherd

Our Shepherd leads us to green pastures and still waters. He leads us in the paths of righteousness. He leads us through the valley of the shadow of death. His rod protects us from predators. His staff guides us along unknown paths. He provides a full table and an overflowing cup. The goodness and steadfast love of the Shepherd accompanies us all through life and ensures that we will dwell in the house of the Lord forever (Psalm 23:2–6).

He does all this for us because we are sheep. It is not a flattering metaphor. We need to be led because we are easily lost. "You were straying like sheep," says the Apostle Peter as he draws an analogy from this proverbial characteristic of sheep (1 Peter 2:25). We're easily confused, easily frightened, easily deceived, prone to wander. We're not terribly smart. We need to be protected because we're utterly defenseless. Sheep lack claws and sharp teeth with which to fight back; they lack tough hides or thick skin that might protect them. They lack speed by which they might flee their attackers, say like a rabbit or deer; they can't escape predators by climbing a tree like a cat or a rocky hill like a goat. Sheep are shiftless, unable to find food, forage, or feed themselves; they are extremely vulnerable. We are sheep. The devil prowls about us like a roaring lion that he might devour us (1 Peter 5:8).

Good shepherd

Jesus is not a hireling. He is the "Good Shepherd" who "lays down his life for the sheep" (John 10:11, 14). He is "the Shepherd and Overseer of (our) souls" (1 Peter 2:25). He wards off the wolves even at the expense of His own life, fulfilling the ideals of the 23rd Psalm (John 10:8–15). What could be more comforting than to know that Jesus the Good Shepherd is there to protect and provide, to lead and to guide His people? He does so providentially, by ordering events to our benefit (Romans 8:28). He does so through His Holy Spirit, who leads the people of God (Romans 8:14). He does so through His word, which is a lamp to our feet and a light to our path (Psalm 119:105). He also does so by placing us in His fold (John 10:1–7), His flock (John 10:16), the equivalent of what we earlier saw was described as a family, a household, a church.

Jesus also leads and provides and protects His people through His undershepherds. He directs Peter and his successors, that is, all ministers of the gospel, to "feed my lambs" and "tend my sheep" (John 21:15–17). Through Peter He directs the elders of the church:

> shepherd the flock of God that is among you, exercising oversight, not under compulsion, but willingly, as God would have you; not for shameful gain, but eagerly; not domineering over those in your charge, but being examples to the flock. (1 Peter 5:2–3)

Note, we are not alone. We are sheep in a flock. The elders shepherd the flock. We draw strength and security not only from our shepherds, but from each other.

Suffering

Yet there is more. Jesus is not only the Good Shepherd, and we His sheep, He is also Himself the Lamb of God who takes away the sin of the world (John 1:29).

> He was oppressed, and he was afflicted,
> yet he opened not his mouth;
> like a lamb that is led to the slaughter,
> and like a sheep that before its shearers is silent,
> so he opened not his mouth. (Isaiah 53:7)

Jesus' example of silent suffering is meant to be a model for us. We too are sacrificial lambs. The Apostle Paul applies Psalm 44:2 to believers.

As it is written, "For your sake we are being killed all the day long; we are regarded as sheep to be slaughtered." (Romans 8:36)

We are "sheep to be slaughtered." We too are called to suffer. Jesus left us an "example" of suffering. We are to "follow in his steps" (1 Peter 2:21):

He committed no sin, neither was deceit found in his mouth. When he was reviled, he did not revile in return; when he suffered, he did not threaten, but continued entrusting himself to him who judges justly. (1 Peter 2:22–23)

We are not only sheep. We are sacrificial lambs, called to suffer. "Through many tribulations we must enter the kingdom of God" (Acts 14:22). "All who desire to live a godly life will be persecuted" (2 Timothy 3:12). This, too, is a vital part of our identity—we are sheep: weak, foolish, needy, vulnerable, oppressed; yet protected, provisioned and led by the Good Shepherd and His undershepherds. We are part of a "flock," whose members provide mutual care and accountability.

What am I? Who am I? I am a *son* of God and a *sibling* of fellow believers. I am also a *sinner* and a *saint*. I am also a *sheep* of God's fold. These "s's" are not a mere mnemonic device, but five principles of the Christian's core identity. As we keep these core ingredients in dynamic tension, they give shape to a Christian's healthy self-concept. I'm a *son* of God, and therefore privileged, protected, and provisioned. I'm a *sibling* and therefore responsible for and accountable to my fellow believers. I'm a *sinner*, and therefore humble and I live in a state of constant dependence. Yet I am also a *saint*, safe and secure, with a destiny that is as certain as God's determination to have me. I am a *sheep*, needy yet guarded by the Good Shepherd.

8. Our Active Identity:

Servants, Subjects, Students

Martyn Lloyd-Jones counsels in his marvelous book *Spiritual Depression,* "Remind yourself of what you are."[1] The Apostle Paul says, "By the grace of God I *am what I am*" (1 Corinthians 15:10). What matters is what God has made us and who we now are because of Christ. "Talk to yourself, remind yourself of ... who you are and what you are, and of what Spirit is within you," Lloyd-Jones counsels.[2] As we move from our "core" identity, we move now to our identity *in action.* If son (and sibling), sinner, sheep and saint describe what we *are,* servant, subject, and student describe the *doing* part of our identity. Certainly there is overlap in these aspects of identity. There is plenty of doing that is implied by sonship, as well as our self-awareness as sinners and saints, but there is a difference in emphasis. The "core" tends more towards the passive, the "given" aspect of our identity, the "active" more towards the duties of our calling.

Servants

Recall our injured lawyer. Not only is he still a *son*, but also a *servant.* Because he is a son, he doesn't cease to be servant. You may wonder about what the Lord said, "No longer do I call you servants (*douloi*) ... *but I have called you friends*" (John 15:15a). His meaning was, "no longer do I call you *merely* servants." Now we are much more than servants, yet without ceasing to be servants. Several verses later He refers to His disciples as ... servants! "A servant is not greater than his master" (John 15:20). Jesus' meaning may also be quite strictly, "I will not *call* you servants," that is, name you as such or treat you as such. Whereas a servant "does not know what his master is doing," he is left in the dark, Jesus doesn't treat His disciples in this way. "For all that I have heard from my Father ... I have made known to you" (John 15:15b). Jesus doesn't *call* us servants yet we still are servants of God.

Similarly the Apostle Paul says, "You are no longer a slave (*doulos*) but a son" (Galatians 4:7). Here the point is that the believer is not a slave of the law, under its ceremonial requirements and its condemnation, the "weak and worthless elementary principles of the world," such as observing "days and months and seasons and years" (Galatians 4:9–10), and requiring circumcision (Galatians 5:2–4). These, plus the cleansing ordinances and dietary laws (Colossians 2:21; 1 Timothy 4:3–5), are a "yoke of slavery" from which Christ has set us free (Galatians 5:1). We are His sons, not slaves of the law.

However, this does not mean that we are not still rightly and properly slaves of God. The Apostle Paul in Romans 6:15–23 presents the Christian life as an exchange of masters. Those who were once slaves of sin "have become *slaves of righteousness*" (Romans 6:17–19). Believers are those who "have been set free from sin and have become *slaves of God*" (Romans 6:22). Divine servitude is not an afterthought or minor theme for the Apostles. It is fundamental to the Christian's experience, even as "servant" or "slave" is central to the Christian's identity. The Apostles constantly identify themselves as bond-slaves (*douloi*) of Christ (see references in ch. 2) or, as we learn further, as servants (*diakonoi*, from which we get our word "deacon") of Christ (Matthew 23:11; Mark 9:35; John 12:26; Romans 16:1), often translated "minister" in the KJV (see Matthew 20:26; Romans 15:8; 1 Corinthians 3:5; 2 Corinthians 3:6; 6:4; 11:15,23; Ephesians 3:7; 6:21; Colossians 1:7,23,25; 4:7; 1 Thessalonians 3:2; 1 Timothy 6:4). Even if bedridden, our struggling lawyer is still able to serve Christ. Even if confined to a wheelchair, he still can please God through service. Our ambition and goal is to serve our master, whatever our condition.

Understanding our identity as servants is crucial to Christian contentment. What does a servant or slave do? Whatever his master assigns for him to do. Listen to the Apostle Paul.

> For am I now seeking the favor of men, or of God? Or am I striving to please men? If I were still trying to please men, I would not be a bond-servant of Christ. (Galatians 1:10)

Because he is a servant of Christ, his aim is to please Christ. If he were "trying to please man," he would be a servant of man and "not a *servant* of Christ." It is a central characteristic of a servant that he aims to please the one he serves, in whatever capacity he is called to do so (see 2 Corinthians 5:7).

It may be that we are forced by circumstances to serve in a diminished capacity. We may have physical or mental limitations. It may be that all our contributions are private, not public. It may be that humanly speaking our service is minor and unimportant. These things are are in our Master's hands. It is true that God decides how, when, and where we serve, but to serve at all is the greatest of life's privileges.

We are "stewards" (another "s"!) of the resources distributed to us by our Master (1 Corinthians 4; 1 Peter 4:10; 1 Corinthians 9:17; Ephesians 3:2; Colossians 1:25). It may be that we are blessed with five talents, or two, or only one. The "good and faithful *servant*" is one who is "faithful" in that which has been entrusted to him (Matthew 25:14–30; Luke 19:11–27).

Yet another way of understanding our servant identity is found in Ephesians 5:25–32. There the Apostle Paul speaks of us, all of us, the church and all its members as the *spouse* (continuing our "S's), or more exactly, the wife of Christ. "When you think about the core of your identity," says David Powlison with some hyperbole, "you are first and foremost *wife*." Christ is husband and Lord. "He is head, leader, master, and dominant partner ... We are subjects, followers, and dependents." "Each of us," Powlison maintains, "in our core identity is meant to live as a subordinate."[3]

I spent four years trying to climb out of the athletic hole in which I was placed by my broken and re-broken right femur. After two years I was back on top of the world, in excellent shape as my senior baseball season started, only to contract pneumonia. Two-thirds of our scheduled games were lost to me. I came back strong in my freshman year at the University of Southern California, but was unable to sustain my success, badly spraining my ankle the following year. I went to my coach and told him of my vision to use the platform of baseball to be a Christian witness, like my close friend and star pitcher Jeff Reinke had, who eventually was drafted by the Detroit Tigers. My coach, a Christian, kindly and gently reminded me that we all have our callings, and Jeff's might not be mine. Much as I might wish to serve Christ as a star pitcher, it was not the will of my Father.

Years ago a young woman came to me for counsel. She was at the end of her twenties with no marital prospects in sight. She was becoming bitter, if not angry, that God had not provided for her. My first counsel to her (but not my last) was that she must embrace the fact that it might not be the will of her Father in heaven for her to marry. That was not the life that she had envisioned. It was not the life that she had wanted. However, it might be her calling. Her peace, joy, and contentment in life would be wrapped in her willingness to accept her role in God's kingdom as a single woman, if that proved to be the will of God.

As we age we have to face the reality of our diminishing capacities for public service and our declining importance in the community and church. We are not able to keep up. We can't hear as much of what's being said. We lack energy. Our opinions don't seem to count as much. Our counsel is less frequently sought. We can struggle with our desire to contribute and our increasingly limited opportunities to do so.

Undoubtedly, the Apostle Paul lamented being trapped in a Roman prison. Without question he wanted to be free to travel about, planting churches and strengthening existing churches. Life in prison was not the life he would have chosen. Yet it was the life that our sovereign God appointed, and as he embraced his circumstances he found contentment. "I have learned," he said, "in whatever situation I am in to be content" (Philippians 4:12). Much as we might wish to serve Christ as successful businessmen or respected professionals, as beloved parents and spouses, as young healthy, whole, and attractive people, it may be the will of God for us to serve flat on our backs in a hospital bed, single, childless, old and poor, and without notable accomplishments.

Robertson McQuilkin enjoyed a dynamic public ministry, serving as a president of Columbia Bible College and Seminary, as a writer, and as a frequent conference speaker. Yet at the height of his influence and peak of his powers, he retired from public life in order to care for his ailing wife. "Living by Vows" was how he explained his decision in an article in *Christianity Today* (October, 1990), and later in a book entitled *A Promise Kept*. Undoubtedly this was a turn of events that he would not have chosen. He would have wished for his wife to remain healthy, for them to continue in ministry together, for them to continue to make their considerable impact on the progress of the kingdom of God. Yet it was not to be. The decision to step down and step back "though painful, was one of the easiest," he explained. Why? Because the decision was made forty two years prior, "when I promised to care for Muriel 'in sickness and in health … till death do us part'."[4]

Joni Eareckson Tada, the quadriplegic Christian author and artist, once asked J. I. Packer, "What can I do that is worth anything?" Packer's answer: "You can worship God." None of us, from the least to the greatest, can do anything of more value than that. Whatever happens in life I am still a son and a servant of God. That which fundamentally defines me is left untouched. As I submit to my Father's will, I find peace and joy in fulfilling His purpose for me. The first jolt of a "frowning providence" (Cowper's term) is difficult to receive. Yet as I bow before my Father's wisdom, I find consolation in serving in whatever capacity He assigns, as His son, and servant.

Subjects

Second, we are subjects of our Lord and King. Fundamental to Christian conversion is the receiving of Jesus Christ as Savior *and* Lord. He is not received as Savior now, and sometime, maybe, later received as Lord. This dual decision way of constructing the Christian life, popularized in the mid-twentieth century, has been utterly discredited in recent years, and rightly so. The Apostle Paul in one of his clearest descriptions of conversion speaks of it as believing in the heart that God raised Jesus from the dead and "confess(ing) with your mouth that Jesus is *Lord*" (Romans 10:9). Likewise, the Apostle Peter concluded his powerful Pentecost sermon with a declaration of Lordship:

> Let all the house of Israel therefore know for certain that God has made him both Lord and Christ, this Jesus whom you crucified. (Acts 2:36)

What must we do to be saved? "Believe in the *Lord* Jesus, and you will be saved" (Acts 16:31). What must every tongue confess? "That Jesus Christ is Lord" (Philippians 2:11). Faith is in the *Lord* Jesus Christ. Conversion may even be understood as a response to a sovereign command. The Apostle Paul preached at Athens,

> The times of ignorance God overlooked, but now he commands all people everywhere to repent. (Acts 17:30)

Because He is Lord, He "commands" repentance. He doesn't merely suggest it, or even request it. His disciples are those who obey that command, repent and submit to His rule. The Apostle Paul even identifies lordship as the goal of the whole work of Christ:

> For to this end Christ died and lived again, that he might be Lord both of the dead and of the living. (Romans 14:9)

Kingdom of God

The central theme of Jesus' teaching ministry was the coming of God's kingdom or reign, in Him. It was on this note that He began preaching:

> Now after John was arrested, Jesus came into Galilee, proclaiming the gospel of God and saying, "The time is fulfilled, and the kingdom of God is at hand; repent and believe in the gospel." (Mark 1:14–15; cf. Matthew 4:17)

His *message* was that of the arrival of the kingdom (Matthew 1:ff.; Luke 17:20–37). His *ethics,* as in the Sermon on the Mount, were the ethics of the kingdom (Matthew 5–7). His *parables* were the parables of the kingdom (Mark 4; Matthew 13). His *miracles* were the evidence of the presence of the kingdom (Matthew 12:28). His mission was and is to bring sinners into His kingdom and under His rule. On the one hand, the Apostle Paul can summarize his message as "nothing ... except Jesus Christ and him crucified" (1 Corinthians 2:2). On the other hand, he can also summarize it saying, 'what we proclaim is not ourselves, but Jesus Christ as *Lord*' (2 Corinthians 4:5; cf. Colossians 1:28). Again, he can summarize his message as "testify(ing) to the gospel of the grace of God." Yet he can also describe it as "proclaiming the kingdom" (Acts 20:24–25). Luke summarized the Apostle Paul's message while under house arrest in Rome as proclaiming the kingdom of God and teaching about the Lord Jesus Christ with all boldness and without hindrance. (Acts 28:31; cf. Acts 28:23)

The King

Jesus is King; by faith and repentance we became His subjects. He is "the King of Kings, the Lord of Lords" (I Timothy 6:15). He is not only the supreme Being, but the supreme Governor and Lawgiver (James 4:12; cf. Isaiah 53:22). He is "the great King above all gods" (Psalm 95:3, 5). He is "the Lord of heaven and earth (Acts 17:24). Our God is "a great King over all the earth." He "reigns over the nations" and "sits on his holy throne" (Psalm 47:2, 8; cf. Psalm 97:1ff)). The believer, as a subject of Almighty God, enjoys what William Gurnall calls "the sweet government of Jesus Christ."[5]

King's commands

The Christian identity as "subject" is highlighted in 2 John 4–6.

> I rejoiced greatly to find some of your children walking in the truth, just as we were commanded by the Father. And now I ask you, dear lady—not as though I were writing you a new commandment, but the one we have had from the beginning— that we love one another. And this is love, that we walk according to his commandments; this is the commandment, just as you have heard from the beginning, so that you should walk in it.

Note the prominent role played by the word "commandment" (*entolē*) in these verses. The word "commandment" or "commanded" occurs four time in these three verses. "The Christian life," says Stott, "*is here viewed from the standpoint of commandments.*"[6] Apparently, this is a valid perspective, not a legalistic one. Who are we? We are subjects who obey our Lord's commands.

Most of us would be unlikely to follow the Apostle's example of describing the Christian life in terms of commandments to obey. We are right to fear misunderstanding. We are right to fear legalism. Many, many people wrongly view Christianity as no more than a list of "do's and don'ts." They see it as no more than a collection of rules, of things required and things forbidden. Too many miss the big picture. Christianity is a religion of grace. We are saved by faith not works; by grace not law; and by Christ not religious performance. Salvation is a gift

God gives, not a wage that we earn (Romans 6:23; Ephesians 2:8–9).

How about once we're saved? What next? Even then the Christian life doesn't become rule-driven. We respond to the gift of salvation with gratitude. We want to honor and serve so gracious a God. It is the "love of Christ" that "constrains" (NASB) or "controls" us (2 Corinthians 5:14). As we've seen, Christ loves us and we, in response, want to please Him. Indeed, it is our ambition (2 Corinthians 5:9). Gratitude motivates our service and obedience. We want to know God and enjoy His fellowship, finding that of "surpassing value" (Philippians 3:8–10). Consequently, we engage in those things that *promote* that fellowship (e.g. Bible reading, prayer, attendance at public services) and avoid those things that *inhibit* it (sin in all its forms). The "those things" are just the details, not oppressive duties or burdensome commandments (1 John 5:3).

The Christian life, we are eager to emphasize, is basically simple. We want to honor our Creator Father and His Savior Son. We are not attempting to earn the favor of God, which is impossible. Our motive arises not from what we are obligated to do, but from what God has already done for us in Christ.

Furthermore, we are right to recognize that ordinarily the apostles speak of the Christian life as a life of faith: we walk (we live) by faith (2 Corinthians 5:7; Galatians 2:20); we stand by faith (Romans 11:20); we wield the shield of faith (Ephesians 6:16). Ian Hamilton has written of *The Faith Shaped Life.* "The Christian life," he rightly says, "from beginning to end is a life of faith."[7] We are also right to emphasize the Christian life as a life of grace. This has been a prominent theme in churches in recent years. Various ministries have been concerned to be "grace-based," and rightly so. We are saved by grace and depend upon God's grace every moment that we live (Ephesians 2:8–9; 2 Corinthians 12:9–10).

Still, the Apostle John is not shy about describing the whole Christian life as a life of subjects who obey our Lord's commands. The Christian life may rightly and properly be described in terms of such. We are commanded to *believe.* The Apostle John urges us to "walk" in the "truth" as "commanded by the Father" (2 John 4). We are commanded to *behave* as well. *Love*, normally an attitude of the heart, is viewed by the Apostle as a commandment (2 John 5). He repeats himself, in case we missed the point: "walk according to his commandments" (2 John 6b). "The knowledge of God as our sovereign King," says Richard Baxter, "must bring the whole man in subjection to him."[8]

Obedience of faith

Maybe this way of discussing the Christian life is not so unusual. The Apostle Paul can summarize his gospel as "*obedience* of faith," which he does twice (Romans 1:5; 16:26), and can speak of conversion as "slaves of sin" becoming "*obedient* from the heart to the standard of teaching to which we were committed" (Romans 6:17). Faith may be viewed as a command to be obeyed. On the day of the revelation of our Lord Jesus, vengeance is promised for "those who do not know God." Yet they are also characterized as "those who do not *obey* the gospel of our Lord Jesus" (2 Thessalonians 1:8). Likewise, Luke describes the conversion of many of Jerusalem's priests in similar language. They "became *obedient* to the faith (Acts 6:7). Jesus even mingles the language of "works" with "faith." "This is the work of God," He says, "that you believe in him whom he has sent" (John 6:29). His disciples are those who hear Jesus' words and *do* them (Luke 6:46–47; 8:21; 11:28). The last book in the Bible repeats twice that they are blessed who "hear" the words of its prophesy and "*keep* what is written" (Revelation 1:3; 22:7). The "offspring" of the woman of Revelation 12 (i.e. the church), that is, members of the church, are characterized simply as "those who *keep the commandments of God* and hold to the testimony of Jesus" (Revelation 12:17; cf. 14:12).

There is a richness to the variety of ways in which Jesus and the Apostles speak of the Christian life. We need not fear the language of obedience if the Apostles don't fear using it. We are commanded to believe, to obey, to trust, to fear, to honor, and to love. Why? Because we are subjects of our Lord and King.

Students

What are the implications of God revealing Himself through prophets and Apostles rather than artists, sculptors, or dramatists? What are the implications of God leaving a permanent *written* record of His saving acts rather than a *visual* one consisting of pictures, statues, symbols, and plays? We have come full circle. Who am I? I am a "disciple" (from the Latin, *dicipulus*, meaning pupil, learner) of Christ. Disciple (*mathētēs*) is the most common title given to the followers of Jesus in the gospels (e.g. 74 times in Matthew) and Acts (30 times). A disciple is a student of another. A disciple is a learner. A disciple is one who sits at the feet of another and learns. The Pharisees had their disciples (Mark 2:18, cf. John 9:28), John the Baptist had his (Mark 2:18; John 1:35), and Jesus called His: first the Twelve, and then all believers thereafter (Luke 6:12–16; Acts 6:1f.).

Jesus is our Teacher as well as our Lord (John 13:13). Disciples have enrolled in the school of Christ. "Take my yoke upon you and *learn* of me," Jesus says (Matthew 11:29). The yoke of discipleship is the yoke of learning. A "disciple" is one who has "learned (*manthanō*) Christ" (Ephesians 4:20). The Apostle describes believers as learners when contrasting them with the sensuality and impurity of pagans. He catalogues the Gentiles' "futility" of mind, their "darkened" understanding, and their "ignorance" and hardness of heart (Ephesians 4:17–18). "But that is not the way you *learned* Christ," he insists. Disciples are those who have "*heard* about him and were *taught* in him, as the truth is Jesus" (Ephesians 4:20–21).

My father earned his Ph.D. in Psychology in 1972 at the University of Southern California (U.S.C.) at the age of 51, the year before I enrolled as a freshman. I recall as a teenager seeing him at his desk for long hours, reading, writing, and typing. I remember thinking that no existence could possibly be more miserable than his. I hated studying. I hated reading. I'd rather dig ditches. I'd rather do manual labor, or so I thought.

Love and learning

Yet I also spent hours and hours of my youth reading and pondering books about World War II. I recall reading in high school for fun Shirer's massive *The Rise and Fall of the Third Reich*. I especially loved the war books with photographs. I would return to them again and again. I knew more about the war than any of my teachers, though I never took a class on it. In fact, in college I argued with my International Relations professor that the betrayal of Czechoslovakia at Munich in 1938 was a military disaster for the Western Allies. He insisted it was inconsequential. I argued that the Czechs had a well-trained army of 30–40 divisions, excellent border fortifications, and a modern armament industry concentrated in the Sudetenland, all of which was lost or neutralized. He was never friendly to me again.

My point? *All of us like to "study" that which we love.* "Every man goes where his love carries him," says the old Latin proverb.[9] Some of the more under-motivated students I know devour the sports page. A disciple of Christ loves Christ and consequently will want to learn everything about Him. Another Latin proverb says, "He that is not zealous does not love."[10] What might otherwise be tedious bookwork becomes exciting and timeless when we love the subject. My spiritual awakening during my sophomore year at U.S.C. transformed my academic career. Every academic subject was now related to Christian discipleship. I was endlessly fascinated by history, psychology, English, Greek mythology. Each subject became a window into which I could more clearly see the truth of God.

Love and appetite

Moreover, once awakened, my appetite for Scripture was insatiable. I read, meditated, and studied not because it was a *duty* external to me but a *desire* within me. Listen to the psalmist:

> Oh how I love your law! It is my meditation all the day. (Psalm 119:97)

> Your testimonies are my heritage forever, for they are the joy of my heart. (Psalm 119:111)

These statements are repeated over and over (e.g. Psalm 119:113, 127, 140, 159, 163, 167). The Law of God is his "delight" (Psalm 119:174). It contains "wondrous things" (Psalm 119:18), and he "longs" for it (Psalm 119:40). Often in our Sunday services we join the psalmist in singing of God's word,

More to be desired are they than gold, even much fine gold; sweeter also than honey and drippings of the honeycomb. (Psalm 19:10)

Disciples as "students" may evoke memories of pale green classrooms, tedium, screeching chalk on blackboards, and endless sitting. We must banish these images from our minds. We devour Scripture because God implants in our hearts a passion for Scripture. We desire God's word more than gold; it is sweeter to our taste than the honeycomb. "Love to God will make the soul inquisitive to find out what is near and dear to God," Gurnall insists.[11]

Pursuing wisdom

Nevertheless, study is necessary. We are to meditate on God's word "day and night" (Psalm 1:2). Only as we "do (our) best," or are "diligent" (NASB), or "study" (KJV) are we able to "rightly handle the word of truth" ("handle accurately" in the NASB, 2 Timothy 2:15). Wisdom must be pursued. A whole book of the Bible is dedicated to the theme of wisdom (Proverbs), not to mention the Apostle Paul's prayers for his churches (Philippians 1:9–11; Ephesians 1:3–23; Colossians 1:3–12). Make your ear "attentive to wisdom" and "incline your heart to understanding," we are urged. "Call out for insight and raise your voice for understanding ... seek it like silver and search for it as for hidden treasure" (Proverbs 2:1–4). "The fear of the Lord is the beginning of wisdom, and knowledge of the Holy One is "insight" or "understanding" (NASB) (Proverbs 9:10; cf. 1:7). Only as we come to know God will we come to properly fear Him and become wise.

We will never become proper disciples passively. Learning doesn't take place by osmosis. I fantasized in college that if I placed my books under my pillow I'd absorb their content in my sleep but it never happened. "Get wisdom; get insight," we are urged (Proverbs 4:2). "Prize her highly" (Proverbs 4:8; see also 4:20–21; 5:1–2; 6:20–23; 7:1–5; etc.).

Jesus envisions His disciples so studying His words that they are able to build their lives upon them (Matthew 7:24–27). Remember, what the gospels present predominately is Jesus as Teacher, whether the Sermon on the Mount, the Sermon on the Plain, the parables, His Olivet and Upper Room discourses, and His various encounters with groups and individuals. He is revealed as the Word, the Divine *Logos*, who was in the beginning with God and was God and became flesh and dwelt among us (John 1:1, 14). That God reveals Himself as the Word; that God reveals Himself through prophets and apostles who speak; and He ensures that a permanent written record of His self-revelation be preserved throughout history. He does so that His saving acts might come to life again, are facts not to be overlooked. We are the "people of the book," as it has been often said. The drift of our civilization away from the typographic to the pictographic, from words to images, is a development to be viewed with concern and resisted.[12] Jesus calls disciples as students and urges that His words not be heard in vain but fully implemented.

Everyone then who hears these words of mine and does them will be like a wise man who built his house on the rock. (Matthew 7:24)

It may be that some of us need to get more disciplined about private Bible reading and study, about reading Scripture with the family, about participation in Sunday School, and about attendance at morning and evening Sunday worship. I have yet to meet a mature Christian who was not an eager student of God's word. Even as a loving husband is a student of his wife, that he might live with her "in an *understanding* way" (1 Peter 3:7), so also loving disciples will study Christ "in all the Scriptures," that they might know all that might be known about Him (Luke 24:27).

9. Our Contrary Identity:

Sojourners, Sportsmen, Soldiers

We move along now from our core identity and our active identity to our *identity in conflict*. The Apostles frequently define believers in contrast with the world. We are in *tension* with the world, in *competition* with it, and even in *combat* with it. Hence we are identified as sojourners, as athletes, and as soldiers. We are not of the world, but aliens, out of step, embattled, fighting for our survival.

> But our citizenship is in heaven, and from it we await a Savior, the Lord Jesus Christ, who will transform our lowly body to be like his glorious body, by the power that enables him even to subject all things to himself. (Philippians 3:20–21)

Sojourners

One of our young summertime missionaries returned to the United States struck by the sense that she was not at home in this world. While in Uganda, she was homesick for Savannah. Back in Savannah, she was not quite comfortable either. Nowhere felt like home anymore.

Her experience reminded me of my first summer in California after an academic year in England. I had been desperately homesick while overseas, barely sustained by the occasional phone call and the periodic letter from family and friends. For months I eagerly anticipated going home. The walk from the arrival gate down the long corridors of Los Angeles International Airport to my waiting family was about the most emotional moment of my entire life. My exile was finally over!

It didn't take long to realize that California was not my home any longer either. A year in England at Trinity College with the Rev. Drs. J. I. Packer and J. A. Motyer had radically altered my spiritual sensibilities. I was profoundly alienated from Southern California and American culture. I was especially alienated from American Christianity. Emotionally it was a difficult time. I didn't fit in England; that was for sure. I didn't think I could possibly stomach another rhubarb pie. Neither did I fit in at home in the USA, even in the sun and surf of California. "What is wrong with you?" one of my closest friends asked with frustration. It was hard to pinpoint. I felt bereft of a homeland, like a man without a country.

Exiles

More or less, I've never recovered from this sense of alienation. I don't believe I'm meant to. "This world's not my home, I'm just a-passin' through," we used to sing in our college Bible studies. Trite, yet it's true. As we mature as Christians we will find more and more that we are not "at home" anywhere in this world because this world is not our home. Heaven is where we really belong. "Our citizenship is in heaven," the Apostle Paul teaches us (Philippians 3:20). We are "sojourners" and "exiles" in this world, both words meaning temporary residents in a foreign place (1 Peter 2:11). Like Abel, Enoch, Noah, Abraham, and Sarah we are "strangers and exiles on earth" (Hebrews 11:13). We are looking with Abraham "to the city that has foundations, whose designer and builder is God" (Hebrews 11:10).

Jesus said, "My kingdom is not of this world" (John 18:36). Consequently, His disciples are hated and persecuted (John 15:18ff). We are misfits, maligned by a mocking world (1 Peter 4:4). An uncomprehending world regards us as "the scum of the world, the refuse of all things" (1 Corinthians 4:13). "The Christian church on earth is always, in a sense, in exile," writes Grove City College Professor Carl R. Trueman. "Whatever the incidental identities of her members—whether of nationality, race, class, or gender," he continues, "their ultimate identity is that they are in Christ and belong to him."[1]

No, we are never quite at home in this world. We are never truly comfortable, never completely at ease. We don't belong *here*, when we step off the airplane, and we don't belong *there* either. Our home is elsewhere. Like the Apostle Paul we long to depart planet earth and be with Christ. We're willing to stay. We'll remain if it's necessary. Yet we know that to depart and be with Christ, to go *home*, is far better (Philippians 1:22–25).

Rejection

This identification of ourselves as pilgrims, as sojourners and exiles, as aliens and strangers, helps us to understand the hostility of the world, as well as our rejection, and our sense of alienation. Jesus warned that if the world hated him it would hate us as well. Why? He explains:

> If you were of the world, the world would love you as its own; but because you are not of the world, but I chose you out of the world, therefore the world hates you. (John 15:19)

We "are not of this world." Consequently, as the world persecuted Jesus, it will persecute us as well (John 15:19).

This alienation from and conflict with the world goes back to the very beginning. Eve gives birth to two sons, Cain her firstborn and Abel. They represent the two humanities—the line of Cain and the ungodly and Abel and the godly. The ungodly line has always persecuted the godly. Cain murders Abel (Genesis 4:2–10). Why did he do it? The Apostle John explains:

> We should not be like Cain, who was of the evil one and murdered his brother. And why did he murder him? Because his own deeds were evil and his brother's righteous. (1 John 3:12)

The lesson:

> Do not be surprised, brothers, that the world hates you. (1 John 3:13)

The Apostle's point is that the conflict goes on. We are not to be surprised if the world hates us because our deeds are righteous, as God counts righteousness, while its are evil. These two lines have continued through history: the godly from Abel, Seth, Enoch, Noah, Abraham, Isaac, Jacob to Jesus to us. We are of the line of Seth. We do not belong to the line of Cain.

Moses, we are told, had something of an identity crisis as an adult. He had been reared in Pharaoh's household with all the privileges and material benefits thereof. Yet he knew who he was and with what people belonged.

> By faith Moses, when he was grown up, refused to be called the son of Pharaoh's daughter, (Hebrews 11:24)

Because he knew his true identity as one of God's people

superseded his identity in the Egyptian royal family, he made a choice. He determined

> rather to be mistreated with the people of God than to enjoy the fleeting pleasures of sin. (Hebrews 11:15)

What was the decisive factor in the decision? His identity was one of God's people and consequently, he chose "to be mistreated with the people of God" rather than enjoy "the fleeting pleasures of sin."

Returning to Rosaria Butterfield, once she converted to Christ she was ostracized by her former associates and friends. "My colleagues and students treated me with suspicion and confusion ... friends felt betrayed, exposed, and criticized by my conversion." The result was "enemies (were made) out of former allies" and "friendships and allegiances" were destroyed. Her summation: "The exclusivity of Christ has rugged consequences."[2]

When I became a serious Christian midway through my sophomore year of college, I quickly was alienated from many of the members of my social fraternity. Some of them were even hostile. They resented what I had come to represent and were happiest when I was not around. Who am I? I am "not of this world."

Separation

Our identity as sojourners means not only *rejection* by the world, but *separation* from the world; not only are we victims of rejection, but active agents removing ourselves from its corruptions. Collectively we are meant to be an outpost of heaven. We are resident aliens, citizens of a distant city, temporarily living in a foreign land, but manifesting the habits, customs, manners, and morals of our home country (Philippians 3:20). Our behavior must match our citizenship.

This means a degree of separation. Gurnall warns us: "If we mean not to be burned, let us not walk upon the coals of temptation."[3] The Apostle urges us,

> Do not be unequally yoked with unbelievers. (2 Corinthians 6:14a)

He asks us rhetorically,

> For what partnership has righteousness with lawlessness? Or what fellowship has light with darkness? What accord has Christ with Belial? Or what portion does a believer share with an unbeliever? What agreement has the temple of God with idols? For we are the temple of the living God. (2 Corinthians 6:14b–16a)

There must be no yoking together of the believer and unbeliever, no "partnership," no "fellowship," no "accord," no "portion," and no "agreement." We are to be ethically and religiously separate, which means there must be a measure of physical and social separation as well.

> Therefore go out from their midst, and be separate from them, says the Lord, and touch no unclean thing; then I will welcome you, and I will be a father to you, and you shall be sons and daughters to me, says the Lord Almighty. (2 Corinthians 6:17–18)

We are to "go out from" and "be separate from them." Gurnall asks us,

Who will sit in the company of drunkards, frequent the places where the sin is committed, and yet pretend they mean not to be such?—that will prostitute their eyes to unchaste objects and yet be chaste?[4]

We are to hate "even the garment stained by the flesh" (Jude 23). This is the opposite of toying with evil. We are to flee from and not to flirt with even the inanimate objects associated with evil (1 Corinthians 6:18; 1 Timothy 6:11; 2 Timothy 2:22). "Bad company corrupts good morals," the Apostle Paul warns us again (1 Corinthians 15:33). Loving our neighbors and enemies means that the separation is not absolute. Evangelistic effectiveness requires a measure of mingling (1 Corinthians 5:9–10). Yet the primary hub of fellowship for the believer, if he or she is to thrive, must be believers, not unbelievers. If my social circle consists primarily of worldlings, it is likely that I will come to resemble them in my priorities, perspective, manners, morals, and behavior. A degree of separation is vital.

Friendship with the world is impossible (James 4:4). Love of the world is destructive (1 John 2:15–17). Knowing this helps us to shape our expectations and cope.

Community

Rod Dreher caused quite a stir with the publishing of *The Benedict Option*.[5] He argues that western civilization has reached a degree of hostility towards and opposition to Christianity that has not been seen since the early centuries of the church. Monasticism (the "Benedictine Rule"), radical separation, was the response then and a monastic-like response is called for now. By this he means not a withdrawal into cloistered communities practicing celibacy, but the creation of our own alternative institutions. We certainly must have our own churches with strong community. Yet we must also have our own schools. No longer can we send our children into public kindergartens and elementary schools in which "Heather has two mommies" will be normalized. No longer can we send our children into schools in which gender is considered "assigned" rather than given, fluid rather than binary, where biological boys might actually be girls and where biological girls might actually be boys. We also will have to create and build our own artistic organizations, media organizations, publishing houses, professional associations. We will have to agree to move into the same neighborhoods and live not in isolation from the world, yet certainly in close proximity to each other. Collectively we must be responsible for each other and accountable to each other that we might be that city set on a hill, that light that shines in the world's darkness that Jesus calls for us to be (Matthew 5:14–16). Isolated we are doomed. The world is too enticing, its lusts too seductive. Collectively we can encourage each other to stand firm in opposition to the world, that we might win the world to Christ and, like the early monks, transform civilization itself.

Sportsmen

After breaking my leg as a sophomore in high school and missing the entire school year, I limped back for my junior year, making considerable progress between August and the following June. Then, beginning in June, I committed myself to an all-out attempt to play football my senior year.

Regrettably, "sports medicine" was unknown and physical rehab was in its infancy. I received no guidance from the medical community or the football team. My leg muscles had atrophied severely and the joints had stiffened after five months in a body cast, followed by surgery, and three more months on crutches. What was I to do?

I devised my own plan. We lived in Long Beach about six miles from the sand. So mid-June I determined to ride my bike to the beach, alternate running four miles in the deep sand one day, four miles in roughly six inches of water the next, and then ride my bike home. When August arrived and official workouts began, I cut out the bike ride but added a four-hour regimen designed to prepare us for football season, consisting of weight training, agility drills, and by the end of summer, fourteen 40-yard wind sprints and a four-mile run (in which, by the way, I crushed the opposition).

It was all to no avail. The muscle, flexibility, and agility never returned adequately. I couldn't play. I could still function as a baseball pitcher. However, I'd never see a football field again.

Spiritual athletes

"Run in such a way that you may win," the Apostle Paul instructs us (1 Corinthians 9:24 NASB). My attempted comeback was my closest brush with serious athletic training. My regimen may not sound so remarkable today, but my contemporaries thought I was a bit nutty. My effort won me the "Most Inspirational" award on the baseball team, but that was about it. The point is, if I were to be an athlete, rigorous training would be necessary, exacting discipline would be required.

Athletics are an effective window into the character of the Christian life. Regularly the Apostle Paul employs metaphors from the world of sports to teach us about the Christian life. We are like athletes both in training and in competition. The Apostle Paul refers to running (Galatians 2:2), boxing (1 Corinthians 9:26); wrestling (Ephesians 6:12), gladiatorial games (1 Corinthians 4:9; 15:32), and perhaps chariot races (Philippians 3:13–14). The Apostle Paul can even use athletic metaphors to characterize his entire Christian ministry. As he senses the approach of death ("the time of departure"), he sums up his service of Christ like this: "I have fought the good *fight*," likening life and service to a boxing match; "I have finished the *race*," now likened to a running event; together meaning, "I have kept the faith" (2 Timothy 4:7). As we learned in reviewing the military metaphors, those who imagine the Christian life to be a quiet, passive, unstressful existence have gotten things exactly wrong. What do athletic metaphors teach us? We can answer our question most clearly from 1 Corinthians 9:24–27 as the Apostle Paul urges total commitment to the cause of the gospel.

Intensity

> Do you not know that in a race all the runners compete, but only one receives the prize? So run that you may obtain it. (1 Corinthians 9:24)

Using the illustration of a race, the Apostle points out that only one person wins. The Christian life is like this: we are to singlemindedly pursue victory over lust, victory over sloth, victory over pride, victory over self, with the intensity of one competing in a marathon. *Only one wins.* We are to live the Christian life with that kind of focus, that kind of commitment, that kind of intensity, that kind of determination. "Thanks be to God," says the Apostle, "who gives us victory through our Lord Jesus Christ" (1 Corinthians 15:57). We aim at victory with total abandonment.

Self-control

> Every athlete exercises self-control in all things. They do it to receive a perishable wreath, but we an imperishable. (1 Corinthians 9:25)

Athletes in training have to exercise self-control. The

University of Southern California swim team won four NCAA championships from 1973–76. Some of my best friends were on the team: Joe Bottom, Rod Stewart, John Naber, Scott Brown, Greg Womble, and a number of others. They swam every morning from 6–8 a.m. and then came to breakfast. Every morning they had to resist the temptation to hit the alarm, roll over, and go back to sleep. They ate a disciplined diet. They slept regular hours. They had to exercise self-control in order to compete.

Does this not speak to the Christian life? "Self-control" is a fruit of the Holy Spirit (Galatians 5:23). If we are to live the Christian life we must discipline our physical appetites, discipline our affections, discipline our devotional life, discipline our commitments. All of this requires "self-control." "I discipline my body and keep it under control," the Apostle continues (1 Corinthians 9:27). Otherwise, if one is responding to every sensuous impulse, indulging anger, lust, sloth, and appetite, one cannot effectively compete and will never win. One's Christian life will forever be out of control. If I want to be a contributing, valued part of the kingdom team, making a difference, my life counting, I will need self-control. I will have to exercise discipline.

Purpose

> Well, I do not run aimlessly, I do not box as one beating the air.
> (1 Corinthians 9:26)

Athletes have a purpose. They have a goal. Runners don't run "aimlessly." They don't run haphazardly all over the countryside. They run on the course. They stay on the track. They run with intention. Similarly boxers don't box the air. They won't win the match by *almost* striking their opponent. They aim to place their fist right on the tip of their opponent's nose. The aim of athletes is to win the race or the match. So also the Christian life. Our rigorous training, our self-denial, our delayed gratification aims at effectively serving Christ. Self-indulgence of some passion or succumbing to the immediate gratification of some lust would be ruinous to our witness and service. Christians must live with focus, pouring all their energy into the race, aiming every punch at the target, which is the honor of Christ, the glory of God, and the salvation of souls. All our resources and energy are poured into this.

Adherence to rules

Commenting on 2 Timothy 2:5, where the Apostle urges that we compete according to the rules, Gurnall insists that we require "not only valor to fight, *but obedience to fight by order and according to the word of command.*"[6] Athletes have to play according to the rules. If they don't, they will be disqualified (1 Corinthians 9:27). If runners, swimmers, or skaters wander out of the lanes, if shot-putters and javelin throwers step over the lines, they are disqualified. The Apostle Paul says elsewhere:

> An athlete is not crowned unless he competes according to the rules. (2 Timothy 2:5)

Christians play according to the rules. What rules? God's rules. He *designed* the games. He *officiates* the games. He is the *umpire*. One might find the lines of the basketball court restrictive; the rule against two-handed dribbling might seem arbitrary; tackling the opponent as he crossed the mid-court line might seem reasonable. However, if we all play according to our own rules, the result is chaos. The whole game shuts down. The game, as an identifiable entity, ceases to exist and gives way to anarchy. So it is for the Christian. It's God's game, God's rules, and God's officiating. Our task is to play by the rules. Rules are good things. They make non-chaotic life possible. Honor the rules.

Reward

Finally, we compete for the reward. The Apostle regularly refers to winning the "prize" (v 24), the "wreath" (v 25, probably the crown of foliage, the *stephanos*, awarded at the Olympic and Isthmian games). Because the Apostle "finished the race," he anticipated receiving "the crown (*stephanos*) of righteousness"

> which the Lord, the righteous judge, will award to me on that Day, and not only to me but also to all who have loved his appearing. (2 Timothy 4:8)

Run to win. Run for the reward. We anticipate not a perishable reward, as are all earthly rewards, but an imperishable. "Therefore," says the writer to the Hebrews:

> since we are surrounded by so great a cloud of witnesses, let us also lay aside every weight, and sin which clings so closely, and let us run with perseverance the race that is set before us, looking to Jesus the pioneer and perfecter of our faith, who for the joy that was set before him endured the cross, despising the shame, and is seated at the right hand of the throne of God. (Hebrews 12:1–2)

Let us then shed "every encumbrance" and every sin "which so easily entangles us," and do what? "*Run* with endurance the *race*" in which we are called to compete (NASB). Who are we? We are sojourners living in tension with the world; we are athletes in competition with the world; and we are soldiers in combat with the world, the flesh, and the devil.

Soldiers

The Puritan William Gurnall (whom we frequently have cited) wrote nearly twelve hundred pages of very small, double-column type on a favorite theme of the Puritans: the Christian life as warfare. His work became a classic: *The Christian in Complete Armour*. Most of the Puritans wrote and preached on the subject, including before him John Downame, *The Christian Warfare* (1608), William Gouge, *The Whole Armour of God* (1627), and after him John Bunyan, *Pilgrim's Progress* (1678), in which the theme of conflict is prominent, and his subsequent work, *The Holy War* (1682). That Gurnall devoted his twelve hundred pages merely to the eleven verses of Ephesians 6:10–20 shows something of the seriousness with which our spiritual ancestors took this theme. The Christian life is a continual warfare, says Gurnall, "from the hour when thou first didst set thy face to heaven, till thou shalt set thy foot in heaven." There is "no condition wherein the Christian is, here below, is quiet … no place which the Christian can call privileged ground."[7]

More recent times have devoted little attention to the subject of the Christian life as warfare, or a Christian's identity as a soldier. One exception might be Martin Lloyd-Jones' wonderful exposition of Ephesians 6:10–20, published in two volumes, entitled *The Christian Warfare* and *The Christian Soldier*.[8] Otherwise the theme has fallen on hard times. Too often the brighter themes of the Christian life have been highlighted at the expense of the tougher. The popular "higher-life" and "victorious life" movements have offered a struggle-free spirituality that leaves little room for spiritual conflict. The promise of uninterrupted peace and joy has squeezed out the martial metaphors and the portrayal of the Christian life as unceasing struggle. Recent decades have shown little patience for life as spiritual warfare.

Yet the Bible employs the military metaphors frequently. God is the "Lord of Hosts," and Lord of armies (e.g. 1 Samuel 1:3, 11; Psalm 24:10; Psalm 46:11; Joshua 5:14–15; Isaiah 1:9; 2:12, etc.). Israel's conquest of the Promised Land (Joshua), its ongoing warfare with its neighbors (Judges–2 Kings), its exile and return (Ezra and Nehemiah) are types or illustrations of the fight of the Christian life. The Apostle refers to believers as "good soldier(s) of Jesus Christ" who must refrain from getting "entangled in civilian pursuits" (2 Timothy 2:4). He urges us to "fight the good fight of faith" (1 Timothy 6:12; cf. 1:18). He urges us to "cast off the works of darkness, and put on the armor of light" (Romans 13:12). The Apostle Peter urges us to "*arm* (our)selves" (1 Peter 4:1), and the Apostle Paul commends "the *weapons* of righteousness" (2 Corinthians 6:7). He teaches us:

> For though we walk in the flesh, we are not waging war according to the flesh. For the weapons of our warfare are not of the flesh but have divine power to destroy strongholds. We destroy arguments and every lofty opinion raised against the knowledge of God, and take every thought captive to obey Christ. (2 Corinthians 10:3–5)

"Waging war," "weapons," "strongholds," "destroy," "captive": this is the apostolic language. If, then, the Christian life is warfare, who is it that we are fighting? We are fighting the trinity of evil: the devil, the world, and the flesh. There is the enemy without and the enemy within. There is the enemy unseen, the enemy seen and around us, and the enemy in our own hearts.

The flesh

Because of the remnants of sin, the believer experiences what the *Confession* calls "a continual and irreconcilable war, the flesh lusting against the Spirit and the Spirit against the flesh" (XIII.2). Flesh and Spirit are "opposed," in conflict with each other (Galatians 5:17). There is within us a law of evil "*waging war* against the law of (our) mind(s) and making us captive(s) of the law of sin" (Romans 7:23). James warns of our "passions (that) are at *war* within (us)" (James 4:1–2). We are locked in a life and death struggle for our souls and the souls of our neighbors.

The devil

The *locus classicus* of Christian warfare is found in Ephesians 6:10–19a:

> Finally, be strong in the Lord and in the strength of his might. Put on the whole armor of God, that you may be able to stand against the schemes of the devil. For we do not wrestle against flesh and blood, but against the rulers, against the authorities, against the cosmic powers over this present darkness, against the spiritual forces of evil in the heavenly places. Therefore take up the whole armor of God, that you may be able to withstand in the evil day, and having done all, to stand firm. Stand therefore, having fastened on the belt of truth, and having put on the breastplate of righteousness, and, as shoes for your feet, having put on the readiness given by the gospel of peace. In all circumstances take up the shield of faith, with which you can extinguish all the flaming darts of the evil one; and take the helmet of salvation, and the sword of the Spirit, which is the word of God, praying at all times in the Spirit, with all prayer and supplication. To that end keep alert with all perseverance, making supplication for all the saints, and also for me.

With whom are we fighting? Not "flesh and blood," meaning

not ultimately that—behind our human "flesh and blood" adversaries are the "cosmic powers over this present darkness," the "spiritual forces of evil," and the "evil one" and his "flaming darts." The devil is our "adversary" who prowls around like a roaring lion seeking someone to devour" (1 Peter 5:8). He schemes (2 Corinthians 2:11) and tempts (1 Thessalonians 3:5) and deceives (2 Corinthians 11:14).

Everything that is vital to the living of the Christian life (e.g. faith, truth, righteousness, prayer, etc.) may be described as a piece of equipment worn by a soldier in battle. Together they constitute the "whole armor of God," the panoply (*pan* = all; *hoopla* = arms) that we are to "take up" (Ephesians 6:13).

The world

We are also in a fight against the world, the "present darkness," the "course of this world," which is controlled by "the prince of the power of the air" (Ephesians 2:2). The world is both hostile and enticing. We are to "love not" the world because "the world is passing away" (1 John 2:15–17; 1 Corinthians 7:31). We are not even to indulge "friendship" with the world (James 4:4). The scriptural testimony is unambiguous. We are in a fight.

Realizing that we live life in a war zone is vital in shaping our expectations. "Nothing is so mischievous as the habit of indulging false expectations," J. C. Ryle warns.[9] "We wrestle," says the Apostle. He uses the present tense. Our fight is lifelong, our spiritual warfare is unceasing. We never arrive at a place where the conflict ends. There is no higher plane, no higher life, no mystical realm where the struggle ends and we can relax. Isaac Watts, in his hymn, "Am I a Soldier of the Cross," asks the question,

Must I be carried to the skies

On flow'ry beds of ease,
While others fought to win the prize,
And sailed through bloody seas?[10]

Warfare requires total commitment. There are no "flow'ry beds of ease" for the soldiers of Christ. Constant vigilance is necessary until the day they put us in the grave. "I toil," says the Apostle, "struggling with all his energy that he powerfully works within me" (Colossians 1:29). Paul labors only because God supplies "his energy," energy which is not meager but which "he powerfully works within me." Yet, the Apostle himself *toils* and *struggles*. "For I want you to know how great a *struggle* I have for you," he continues (Colossians 2:5). The Bible is beautifully balanced. "Who does the fighting?" Lloyd-Jones asks in one of the great chapters in his works.[11] We do. We must put sin to death. Mortification is our responsibility (Romans 8:13; Colossians 3:5). We must resist the devil if we are to see him flee (James 4:7). We must "put on the whole armor of God." We must "stand firm." We must "pray at all times" and "keep alert." Yet we are able to do so only as we are "strong in the Lord and in the strength of *his* might" (Ephesians 6:10). It is not our armor, but *God's*, that we put on. Charles Wesley summarizes our situation beautifully:

Soldiers of Christ arise,
    And put your armor on,
Strong in the strength which God supplies
    Through his eternal Son.
    Strong in the Lord of Hosts,
    And in his mighty pow'r,
Who in the strength of Jesus trusts
    Is more than conqueror.

Stand then in his great might,

> With all his strength endued;
> But take, to arm you for the fight,
>> The panoply of God.
>> Leave no unguarded place,
>> No weakness of the soul;
> Take ev'ry virtue, ev'ry grace,
>> And fortify the whole.[12]

Victory is assured. Why? Again, because the armor that we put on is *God's* armor. For no other reason are we able "to withstand in the evil day" (Ephesians 6:13). Yet with that armor we *are* able to withstand. We are strong only "in the Lord and in the strength of his might" (Ephesians 6:10). Yet in His strength we are strong. "Thanks be to God," says the Apostle Paul, "who give us the victory through our Lord Jesus Christ" (1 Corinthians 15:57). Listen again to Wesley:

> To keep your armor bright,
>> Attend with constant care;
> Still walking in you Captain's sight,
>> And watching unto prayer.
>> From strength to strength go on;
>> Wrestle and fight and pray;
> Tread all the pow'rs of darkness down,
>> And win the well-fought day.[13]

Listen to the promise of the Apostle John:

> For everyone who has been born of God overcomes the world. And this is the victory that has overcome the world—our faith. (1 John 5:4)

By faith in Christ we are able to overcome the world and gain the victory over sin and death. "We are more than conquerors," says the Apostle, victors over all manner of opposition (Romans

8:35–39), "through him who loved us" (Romans 8:37; cf. Revelation 2:11, 17, 26; 3:5, 12, 21). Let us learn to sing gladly,

> Onward, Christian soldiers, marching as to war,
> with the cross of Jesus going on before;
> Christ, the royal Master, leads against the foe;
> forward into battle see his banners go!
>
> At the sign of triumph Satan's host doth flee;
> on then, Christian soldiers, on to victory:
> hell's foundations quiver at the shout of praise;
> brothers, lift your voices, loud your anthems raise.
>
> Like a mighty army moves the church of God;
> brothers, we are treading where the saints have trod;
> we are not divided, all one body we,
> one in hope and doctrine, one in charity.[14]

How encouraged we ought to be. Lust will be conquered. Those outbursts of anger will be defeated. That bad habit or addiction will be overcome. Selfishness, sloth, pride, judgmentalism will all be put to death. Nations will be won. Peoples will be saved. Who are we? We are soldiers of Christ. And we will win the battle against the devil, the world, and our own.

10. Concluding Considerations

Serving and Obeying God

"It requires more prowess and greatness of spirit to obey God faithfully," says Gurnall, "than to command an army of men."[1] Who are we? We are Christians. We are disciples of Christ. How are we to serve and obey Christ? How do these eleven elements of our identity come together to shape our living of the Christian life? We have commented on the practical implications throughout. Can we now summarize what our service and obedience looks like? Stephen Charnock (1628–1680) in his magnificent *Discourses Upon the Existence and Attributes of God,* describes the implications of God's dominion, saying,

> Whatsoever he speaks as a true God, ought to be *believed*; whatsoever he orders as a sovereign God ought to be *obeyed*.[2]

He outlines the characteristics of our obedience and service under several headings, which we may find to be helpful, if only in brief. Long ago the church learned to distinguish between moral, civil, and ceremonial aspects of God's law. The civil laws with civil penalties were designed for Israel as a nation-state. As the people of God are no longer organized as a political entity, those laws no longer have a realm in which they are meant to be applied beyond what the *Westminster Confession of Faith* calls the "general equity thereof" (XIX.4). The ceremonial laws, such as the cleansing laws, dietary laws, circumcision, and the calendar of holy days, were typological in nature and were fulfilled in that to which they pointed, that is, the redemption that is in Christ. For example, we no longer have a temple (John 4:21ff). We no longer have a Levitical priesthood (Hebrews 7:11). We no longer are restricted by dietary and cleansing laws which require "do not handle, do not taste, do not touch" (Colossians 2:16–23; 1 Timothy 4:1–4; Mark 7:19). We no longer observe "days and months and seasons and years" (Galatians 4:10).

The ongoing normativity of the moral law over against the ceremonial law can be seen in the simple statement of the Apostle Paul as he urges Greek believers not to seek circumcision:

> For neither circumcision counts for anything nor uncircumcision, but keeping the commandments of God. (1 Corinthians 7:19 cf. Galatians 6:14)

Was circumcision not commanded? Of course it was. Yet as a ceremonial requirement it can be sharply distinguished from "the commandments of God," that is, the moral law. The moral law continues, the ceremonial law doesn't. "If you love me," Jesus says, "you will keep my commandments" (Jn14:15). What, then, do our obedience and service look like across the spectrum of the various aspects of our identity?

Unqualified

First, our obedience and service is to be *unqualified*. We obey and serve, in the end, not because it is in our interest, or because it promotes our well-being, or because we find it sensible, but because God has required it of us. Of course His demands are in our self-interest. What He requires is for our well-being. What He asks is reasonable (James 3:17, NASB). What Jesus says of the Sabbath command may be said of all of God's commands: they are made "for man," for humanity, for our good (Mark 2:17). His commandments promote the sanctity of life, intact marriages, respect for property, high regard for truth, contentment with what I have, and contentment with what others have that I don't have (see: Commandments 6–10 of the Ten). Yet these are not the reasons why we obey. There may be occasions when we don't understand why He forbids one thing and allows another. There may be times when it seems arbitrary that one thing is prohibited and another is permitted. No matter. Our bottom line is "Thus saith the Lord." No further reason need be given beyond God would have it so. No explanation need be offered—He is God, He is our Father. Jesus Christ is our Lord, He is our King, He is our Master and our Commander. We don't bargain or negotiate, we don't say "I'll obey *if* God will bless me." "I'll serve *if* He gives me what I want." Rather, we obey and serve because God has commanded, because He has the indisputable authority to command, and we have the unqualified obligation to obey. The "proper rule of obedience" says Charnock, is "nothing but the sole power and authority of God."[3]

Precise and excellent

Second, our obedience is to be *precise and our service is excellent.* We are to obey in all of the *details.* We are to render *excellent* service. Why? Because we want to please our Father. We want to honor our Lord and King. He is to receive the best of our labor, not our blemished lambs (Malachi 1:14). God is to receive our best thoughts, our peak energy, our focused attention, not our leftovers; not what remains after we have served our own interests. We *are* to tithe the mint, dill, and cumin (the details) and yet not neglect the weightier matters (the broader principles) of justice, mercy and faithfulness (Matthew 23:23). Our yes is to be yes and our no, no (Matthew 5:37). We are to keep a careful Sabbath. We are to be precise in our obedience, like our Puritan fathers who were scorned as "precisionists." Our yes and no should not slide into a maybe, a later, or sometime. We should be known as reliable, faithful, and dependable because we do just as we say we will, no less. "It is a great honour to a Christian, yea, to religion itself," says Gurnall, "when all their enemies can say is, They are precise, and will not do as we do."[4]

Sincere

Third, our obedience and service are to be *sincere and from the heart.* We are not merely to check the boxes of accomplished tasks. We are not to clock-in and clock-out. God is not pleased with rote, mindless or begrudged obedience and service. "All that is within (us) is to bless His holy name," our affections as well as our actions (Psalm 103:1). We are to worship in spirit as well as in truth (John 4:24). For us to settle for external compliance without regard for the internal attitude is to repeat the errors of the Pharisees whom Jesus described as "whitewashed tombs," clean on the outside while the inside is full of death and corruption (Matthew 23:27–28).

Concern for the external without regard for the internal is also the error of radical Islam. Many of us have wondered why the Islamic radicals use terror tactics which seem unlikely to win adherents and rather more likely to drive potential converts away in horror. What we misunderstand is their aim.

They are not interested in convincing minds and hearts. Islam means "submission." A Muslim is "one who submits." The heart attitude of converts is of little relevance to them. Their aim is to terrorize non-Muslims into submission. Beheadings, kidnappings and suicide bombings are an effective tool in forcing a village, a country, a people to submit. A Christian ordered to renounce Christ and confess Islam or watch his children be beheaded is surely tempted to submit.

The God of the Bible is very different from the god of Islam. He cares about motive. He cares about sincerity. Because He cares, we care. Earnestness matters. He requires willing, glad, joyful obedience. He is to be loved with all our heart, mind, soul, strength (Mark 12:30; Luke 10:27). We believe with the *heart* (Romans 10:9). We sing and worship with the *heart* (Ephesians 5:19). We pray ("draw near") with sincere *hearts* (Hebrews 10:22). We are to be "obedient *from the heart* to that form of teaching to which we were committed" (Romans 6:17). We are to *delight* in God's commandments (Psalm 1:2; 119:24). They are to be desired by us and sweet to us (Psalm 19:10). Because this is what our Father, our Lord and King requires, this is what we want to give, from the heart. "Involuntary obedience deserves not the title" of obedience, warns Charnock: "it is rather submission than obedience, an act of the body not of the mind." Rather, "A mite of obedience with cheerfulness," he insists, "is better than a talent without it."[5] Because God is our Father, it is our joy to serve Him, our ambition to please Him (2 Corinthians 5:9). We "serve the Lord with gladness" (Psalm 100:2).

Final

Fourth, our obedience and service is to recognize that the authority of God is *final*. Jesus said, "him only shall you serve," quoting Deuteronomy 6:13 (Luke 4:8). God is to be obeyed and served above all others. He is to be obeyed above all earthly authorities: "we must obey God rather than men," the Apostle Peter announced to the Jewish council (Acts 5:29). The authority of God's word trumps all alternate sources of authority whether they be political, academic, ecclesiastical, or familial.

Science makes many grandiose claims. We respect science. We appreciate the scientific method. The list of outstanding Christian scientists is long. From the past it included Frances Bacon (1561–1626), author of the scientific method, Johannes Kepler (1571–1630), Isaac Newton (1642–1727), Blaise Pascal (1623–1662), Lord Kelvin (1824–1907), Michael Faraday (1791–1867), James Clerk Maxwell (1831–1879), and today, Henry F. Schaefer, perhaps the leading theoretical chemist in the world, and a long list of others which he describes.[6] However, science's "assured results" are constantly in flux. "Settled science" is an oxymoron. Science is never settled. It is constantly adjusting to new data, as it should. Yet too easily science becomes what C. S. Lewis called "scientism," its present findings received uncritically and defended with religious zeal. When science conflicts with Scripture, we go with Scripture and wait for science to catch up. Why? Because Scripture is God's Word. When Scripture speaks, God speaks. What Scripture says, the all-mighty, all-knowing, and all-wise God says.[7]

The civil government? It also makes expansive claims. It may want Christian organizations and employers to provide health insurance that pays for abortions. It may want to use anti-discrimination laws to force Christian organizations and Christian employers to hire employees without regard to moral considerations or gender issues. It may use "hate speech" laws to silence Christian pulpits in connection with moral issues.

Again, we must obey God rather than men (Acts. 5:24). God's word is the final authority. He is our Father, our Lord, and our King.

Even our obedience to lesser authorities ultimately may be traced back to obedience to God. Children obey parents "in the Lord" (Ephesians 6:1). Slaves obey masters "as to Christ" (Ephesians 6:5). Wives submit to husbands "as to the Lord" (Ephesians 5:22–24). Civil authority is to be obeyed "for the Lord's sake" (1 Peter 2:13; cf. Romans 13:1–7). "The authority of God is to be eyed in all the services payable to man," says Charnock. "What obedience is due to man, is but rendered as a part of obedience to God, and as stooping to his authority."[8] He is our Father. He is our Lord. He is King above all other fathers, lords, and kings.

Universal

Fifth, our obedience and service are to recognize that God's authority is *universal*. All of God's commands are to be obeyed and they are to be everywhere, and all the time. "We are not to pick and choose among his precepts," Charnock reminds us.[9] Human laws have limited application. They are normative in one city and not in another, in one country and not another, at one time and not another. God's laws are authoritative everywhere all the time. Our obedience is to be *perpetual*. We are to obey His commands in all places and at all times. Similarly we are to serve God at all places and at all times. Never are we released from His service. We are ever sons under the authority of our Father. We are ever the servants, ever the slaves of our Lord and King.

The Christian life is more than obedience and service. We are saved by Christ, by grace, through faith (Ephesians 2:8–9).

Yet it is valid to conceive of the Christian life as obedience and service rendered by sons to their Father, by servants to the Lord, by subjects to their King, and in every dimension of our identity. Let us then obey all that our Father, our Lord, and our King commands by *believing* what He says, *behaving* as He requires, and *loving* one another.

Identity and Perspective

We now return to our opening consideration of balance in the Christian life. What happens when one or two aspects of our Christian identity get emphasized at the expense of others? What happens when we fail to keep the five *core* elements (sons, sinners, siblings, sheep, saints), or three *active* elements (servants, subjects, students), or three *contrary* elements (sojourners, soldiers, sportsmen) of our identity in tension with each other?

Passive versus active

Some have made "sons and "saints" the message of the gospel and have neglected the categories of "sibling," "servant," "sinner," "sheep," and "subjects." The result has been a strong emphasis on our unchanging security as children of God and our safe status as "holy ones," righteous in Christ. Many hurting souls have derived great comfort from this constant refrain. Those of "tender conscience," to use the Puritan term, have found deep consolation in regular reminders of sonship and sainthood.

However, in the absence of an ongoing emphasis on "sibling" or "servant," "sinner," "sheep," and "subject," the result too often has been complacency about duty, service, responsibility, and even about sin. "Don't *should* me," some preachers have been known to say. "There is nothing that I *must do* that will make God love me more. There is nothing that I *have done* that will make Him love me less," these preachers rightly insist. Yet, they continue, "My Father is always pleased with me and never displeased. He sees me 'in Christ,' perfect and complete. Consequently, don't tell me what I need to do. I don't need to do anything except just rest in grace. When I fail, I'm loved and accepted. When I fall, I am safe and secure. The Christian life is not *doing* but *being*, being 'in Christ.'"

There is a problem with this even in terms of sonship. While fathers don't *love* their children more or less according to their performance, they may be more or less *pleased* according to service and obedience. We are regularly told to do the things with which God is pleased and that He rewards and blesses (e.g. Matthew 6:1ff; 2 Corinthians 5:9; Colossians 1:10; Ephesians 5:10). God's love is unchanging. However, He may be more or less pleased with us, and may be at times quite displeased.

Beyond this, the larger problem is the emphasis that is being placed on one aspect of our identity (sonship and sainthood) at the expense of the others (sibling, servant, sinner, sheep, and subject). We are called to serve (Romans 12:1–2). I am a son, but I am also a servant, a sibling, and a subject. This means that I have the duties and responsibilities of servants, siblings, and subjects which I am not to neglect. Moreover, while I am a saint, I am also a sinner, sheep and sojourner. I have not yet arrived. I'm not at home. I must "press on," as the Apostle Paul put it (Philippians 3:14). I have not yet been glorified. I am not yet in heaven. I am not in a state of *non posse pecare*. The dregs of sin, weakness, and foolishness that remain can only be overcome by strenuous acts of mortification and vivification, as we have seen. No room is left for complacency.

Err in one direction and I may end up in Vanity Fair with those who are "at ease in Zion" (Amos 6:1). If all I hear is that I am a *son* and a *saint*, I may become flippant about sin and negligent of duty. However, if I err in the other direction, I may sink into the Slough of Despond. If all I hear is that I am a miserable wretch of a *sinner*, or a foolish and helpless sheep, then I am unlikely to experience the joy of forgiveness: justification, adoption, and the certainty of eternal life. If all I hear is that I am a *servant and subject*, then God may become to me an oppressive taskmaster, whose presence is avoided because an awareness of God means still another task added to my already overburdened job description.

Our concept of the Christian's identity must accommodate notions of obedience, duty, responsibility, obligation, and fear. I must not conceive of the Christian life in such a way that excludes these demanding elements of the Christian experience. If I fail to incorporate them into my understanding of what grace gives and requires, then I have formulated a false grace. A concept of Christian identity that excludes obedience, duty, responsibility, obligation, and fear is unknown in the New Testament; it is a Christian life unrecognized by Jesus and the Apostles.

Likewise, I must not allow my concepts of Christian obedience, duty, etc., to undermine the Christian's absolute security. It is the faith of the one "who does not work but believes in Him who justifies the ungodly" that is "reckoned as righteousness" (Romans 4:5). Nothing can "separate us from the love of God, which is in Christ Jesus our Lord" (Romans 8:38–39). We have a divinely given safety, a peace and joy that no one can take away.

Peaceful versus combative

There have also been those who have wanted to define the Christian almost entirely in relation to God and fellow believers while ignoring the world. They have embraced the "core" and "active" elements of the Christian identity. We are sons of God, servants of God, subjects of God, students of God's word, siblings in Christ, and saints/sinners, they have maintained. However, they have implied, at least by omission, that one can be at peace with the world, or ignore the world, and that the world will leave us alone. All we need to do is love one another and serve Christ and all will be well. All our trouble in the world, they assume, is of our own doing, brought on by our own misdeeds.

Certainly we can stir up trouble unnecessarily. The Apostle Peter warns us about this. "If you are insulted for the name of Christ, you are blessed, because the Spirit of glory and of God rests upon you" (1 Peter 4:14). Suffering for the name of Christ is one thing. However, he cautions, "But let none of you suffer as a murderer or a thief or an evildoer or as a meddler" (1 Peter 4:15). "Yet," he cautions, "Yet if anyone suffers as a Christian, let him not be ashamed, but let him glorify God in that name" (1 Peter 4:16).

Conflict with the world is inevitable, as we've seen. We lose sight of this when we neglect our identities as soldiers, athletes, and sojourners. No matter how "nice" we are; no matter how good we are; no matter how loving we are, we are aliens, and we will have conflict with the world for which we must train like athletes to prepare.

J. I. Packer taught me to dislike the word "balance." He called it a "horrible, self-conscious word."[10] We might use a term like "proportionate." Keep these themes of identity in proper proportions. Or we might use a term like "perspective." Don't lose a biblical perspective on these issues. Yet it is balance that we are urging. These elements of our identity must be kept in dynamic tension with each other lest we fall into legalism on the one side, or antinomianism on the other; hyper-activism at the one end, passivity and complacency at the other. We are advocates of *lectio continua* preaching in no small part because it forces preachers to deal with the whole Bible, biblical themes in biblical proportions. As we do so, we avoid the pitfalls of an imbalanced emphasis on one aspect of our identity at the expense of another.

We instinctively do balance the various aspects of our earthly identities. We may be at once a son, brother, father, husband, employee/employer, and American citizen. The Apostle Peter can say without a sense of irony, "Live as people who are *free*, not using your freedom as a cover up for evil," and then with the next breath say, "but living as *servants* of God" (1 Peter 2:16). We are free, but servants (*douloi*, slaves). We wear many hats. Privileges, duties, and responsibilities are constantly shifting. Yet we move effortlessly from one earthly identity to the next, from one earthly obligation to the next, from one earthly opportunity to the next, seamlessly and simultaneously. As we grow in grace, we shall learn to do so respecting our spiritual identities as well.

Bibliography

Baxter, Richard. "A Divine Life," in *The Works of Richard Baxter*, Vol. III. (Ligonier, PA: Soli Deo Gloria, 1990)

Butterfield, Rosaria Champagne. *The Secret Thoughts of an Unlikely Convert: an English Professor's Journey into the Christian Faith* (Pittsburgh, PA: Crown & Covenant Publications, 2012)

—— "What is Wrong with Gay Christianity? What is Side A and Side B Anyway?", www.theaquilareport.com, February 7, 2019

—— *Openness Unhindered: Further Thoughts of an Unlikely Convert on Sexual Identity and Union with Christ* (Pittsburgh, PA: Crown & Covenant Publications, 2015)

—— "An Unlikely Convert: Rosaria Butterfield: An Interview," *Tabletalk*, April 2015, Volume 39, No. 4

Calvin, John. *Institutes of the Christian Religion*, Vols. 1 & 2, in John T. McNeill (ed.), The Library of Christian Classics, Vol. XXI (Philadelphia: Westminster Press, 1960)

Charnock, Stephen. *Discourses Upon the Existence and Attributes of God*, Volumes I and II. (1682: Grand Rapids: Baker Book House, 1979)

Dreher, Rod. *The Benedict Option: A Strategy for Christians in a Post-Christian Nation* (New York: Sentinel, 2017)

Elliot, Elisabeth, *Let Me Be a Woman* (Wheaton, IL: Tyndale House Publishing, Inc., 1976)

Friedrich, Otto. *Blood and Iron* (New York: HarperCollins, 1995)

Gordon, T. David, *Why Johnny Can't Sing Hymns* (Phillipsburg, NJ: P & R Publishing, 2010)

Gurnall, William. *The Christian in Complete Armour* (1662–1665; Edinburgh: The Banner of Truth Trust, 1964)

Hamilton, Ian. *The Faith-Shaped Life* (Edinburgh: The Banner of Truth Trust, 2013)

Johnson, Terry, *The Case for Traditional Protestantism* (Edinburgh: The Banner of Truth Trust, 2004)

—— *The Identity and Attributes of God* (Edinburgh: The Banner of Truth Trust, 2019)

—— *Worshipping with Calvin* (Darlington, England: EP Books, 2014)

Lloyd-Jones, Martin. *Spiritual Depression* (Grand Rapids: William B. Eerdmans Publishing Co., 1965)

—— *The Christian Warfare* (Grand Rapids: Baker Books, 1976)

—— *The Christian Soldier* (Grand Rapids: Baker Books, 1977)

McQuilkin, Robertson. *A Promise Kept* (Wheaton, IL: Tyndale House Publications, Inc., 1998)

Oden, Thomas. *How Africa Shaped the Christian Mind:*

Rediscovering the African Seedbed of Western Christianity (Downers Grove, IL: InterVarsity Press, 2010)

Owen, John. "On the Mortification of Sin in Believers," *Works of John Owen* Vol. VI (1850–53; London: The Banner of Truth Trust, 1966)

Packer, J. I. *A Quest for Godliness: The Puritan Vision of the Christian Life* (Wheaton, IL: Crossway Books, 1990)

—— *Knowing God* (Downers Grove, IL: InterVarsity Press, 1973)

—— "The Trinity and the Gospel," in *Celebrating the Saving Work of God: The Collected Shorter Writings of J. I. Packer*, Vol. 1. (Carlisle, Cumbria, UK: Paternoster Press, 1998)

Postman, Neil. *Amusing Ourselves to Death* (1985; New York: Penguin Books, 2006)

Powlison, David. "How Does Sanctification Work?" (Part 2). *Journal of Biblical Counseling*, 27:2, 2013

—— *Seeing with New Eyes: Counseling and the Human Condition Through the Lens of Scripture* (Phillipsburg, NJ: P & R Publishing, 2003)

Ryle, J. C., *Expository Thoughts on the Gospels* Vol. Four: John 10:10–End (1874: Grand Rapids: Zondervan Publishing House, 1951)

Schaefer III, Henry F. *Science and Christianity: Conflict or Coherence?* (Watkinsville, GA: The Apollos Trust, 2003)

Stott, John. *The Epistles of John: An Introduction and Commentary.* Tyndale New Testament Commentaries. 1964; (Grand Rapids: William B. Eerdmans Publishing Company, 1975)

Trinity Hymnal (Atlanta, GA: Great Commission Publications, 1990)

Trueman, Carl R. "The Church in Exile," *New Horizons*, June 2015

Tucker, Ruth A. *From Jerusalem to Irian Jaya: Biographical History of Christian Missions* (Grand Rapids: The Zondervan Corporation, 1983)

Warfield, B. B. *Perfectionism*, Volumes I and II. (New York: Oxford University Press, 1931)

—— "It says: Scripture Says: God Says," in *The Inspiration and Authority of the Bible* (1929; Philadelphia, PA: Presbyterian and Reformed Publishing, 1948)

Venning, Ralph, *The Sinfulness of Sin* (Edinburgh: The Banner of Truth Trust, 1993 [1669])

Endnotes

Chapter 1. Opening Considerations

1. Cited in Ruth A. Tucker, *From Jerusalem to Irian Jaya: Biographical History of Christian Missions* (Grand Rapids: The Zondervan Corporation, 1983), 115.

2. J. I. Packer, *Knowing God* (Downers Grove, IL: InterVarsity Press, 1973), Chapter 19, 181–208.

3. B. B. Warfield, *Perfectionism*, Volumes I and II (New York: Oxford University Press, 1931).

4. J.I. Packer, "The Trinity and the Gospel," in *Celebrating the Saving Work of God, The Collected Shorter Writings of J. I. Packer*, Vol. 1. (Carlisle, Cumbria, UK: Paternoster Press, 1998), 7.

5. J. I. Packer, *A Quest for Godliness: The Puritan Vision of the Christian Life* (Wheaton, IL: Crossway Books, 1990), 126.

6. David Powlison, "How Does Sanctification Work? (Part 2)," *Journal of Biblical Counseling*, 27:2 (2013).

Chapter 4. Behaviour and Identity

1. Otto Friedrich, *Blood and Iron* (New York: HarperCollins, 1995), xi.

Chapter 5. Mistaken Identity—I

1. Rosaria Champagne Butterfield, *The Secret Thoughts of an Unlikely Convert: an English Professor's Journey into Christian Faith* (Pittsburgh: Crown & Covenant, 2012), ix. She addresses the problem of false identity in her sequel, *Openness Unhindered: Further Thoughts of an Unlikely Convert on Sexual Identity and Union with Christ* (Pittsburgh: Crown and Covenant Publications, 2015).

2. Ibid., 12.

3. Ibid.

4. Ibid., 14.

5. Ibid., 20.

6. Ibid., 16.

7. Ibid., 1.

8. Ibid., 25.

9. Ibid., 27.

10. Ibid., 29.

11. Ibid., 25.

12. Ibid., ix.

13. Ibid., 21.

14. Ibid., 24 (my emphasis).

15. Ibid., 24 (my emphasis).

16. Ibid., 32.

17. Ibid., 33.

18. Ibid., 34.

19. Ibid., 51 (my emphasis).

20. Ibid., 2.

21. Ibid., 108.

Chapter 6. Mistaken Identity—II

1. Thomas C. Odom, *How Africa Shaped the Christian Mind: Rediscovering the African Seedbed of Western Christianity* (Downers Grove, IL: InterVarsity Press, 2010).

2. See present author's *Worshipping with Calvin* (Darlington: EP Books, 2014), pp. 240–295.

7. Our Core Identity

1. William Gurnall, *The Christian in Complete Armour,* (1662–1665; London: The Banner of Truth Trust, 1964), I:323.

2. Gurnall, *Christian in Complete Armour,* I:553.

3. George Swinnock, "The Christian Man's Calling," in *The Works of George Swinnock*, Vol. II (Edinburgh: The Banner of Truth Trust, 1992 [1868]), p. 522. According to Owen, one of the principle means of perpetuating humility among believers is "the remembrance of that woeful defiled state and condition from whence they have been delivered," the remembrance of "what they were and whence they came" (*The Holy Spirit*, Works, Volume III, p. 459; citing Deuteronomy 26:1–5; Ezekiel 16:3–5; Psalm 51:5; Ephesians 2:11–13; 1 Corinthians 6:9–11). He continues: "When they consider what was their natural state and condition—universally leprous and polluted,—with what remainders of it do still abide, it casts them on the earth, and causeth them to lay their mouths in the dust" (Ibid.).

4. Gurnall, *Christian in Complete Armour*, I:478.

5. B. B. Warfield, *Perfectionism*, I:117.

6. Gurnall, *Christian in Complete Armour*, I:478.

7. Ralph Venning, *The Sinfulness of Sin*, Puritan Paperbacks (London: The Banner of Truth Trust, 1965 [1669]).

8. Swinnock, "Christian Man's Calling", *Works*, II:427.

9. Isaac Watts, "Alas! And Did My Savior Bleed," Trinity Hymnal (Atlanta: Great Commission Publications, 1990), #254, stanza 1.

10. Ibid., stanza 2.

11. Swinnock, "The Christian Man's Calling," *Works*, II:427.

12. John Owen, "On the Mortification of Sin in Believers," *Works of John Owen*, Vol. VI. (London: Banner of Truth Trust; 1966), p. 9.

13. Luke describes believers as first being called Christians (by others) in Acts 11:26. Also Agrippa famously says, "Almost they persuaded me to be a Christian" (Acts 26:28).

14. Article 13 of the "Nashville Statement on Human Sexuality" reads, "WE AFFIRM that the grace of God in Christ enables sinners to forsake transgender self-conceptions and by divine forbearance to accept the God-ordained link between one's biological sex and one's self-conception as male or female. WE DENY that the grace of God in Christ sanctions self-conceptions that are at odds with God's revealed will."

15. Rosaria Butterfield, "What is Wrong with Gay Christianity? What is Side A and Side B Anyway?", www.theaquilareport.com, February 7, 2019.

Chapter 8. Our Active Identity

1. D. Martyn Lloyd-Jones, *Spiritual Depression* (Grand Rapids: William B. Eerdmans Publishing Co., 1965), 86.

2. Ibid., 105.

3. David Powlison, *Seeing with New Eyes: Counseling and the Human Condition Through the Lens of Scripture* (Phillipsburg, NJ: P & R Publishing, 2003), 62.

4. Robertson McQuilkin, *A Promise Kept*, (Wheaton, IL: Tyndale House Publications, Inc, 1998), 21–22.

5. Gurnall, *Christian in Complete Armour*, I:158.

6. John Stott, *The Epistles of John: An Introduction and Commentary,* Tyndale New Testament Commentaries (1964; Grand Rapids: William B. Eerdmans Publishing Co., 1975), 207 (my emphasis).

7. Ian Hamilton, *The Faith Shaped Life* (Edinburgh: The Banner of Truth Trust, 2013), 9.

8. Richard Baxter, "A Divine Life," in *The Works of Richard Baxter,* Vol. III (Ligonier, PA: Soli Deo Gloria, 1990), 800.

9. *Amor meus pondus meum.*

10. *Ad ultimum sui possee.*

11. Gurnall, *The Christian in Complete Armour,* I:312.

12. See Neil Postman, *Amusing Ourselves to Death* (1985; New York: Penguin Books, 2006).

Chapter 9. Our Contrary Identity

1. Carl R. Trueman, "The Church in Exile," *New Horizons*, June 2015.

2. "An Unlikely Convert: Rosaria Butterfield: An Interview," *Tabletalk*, April 2015, Volume 39, No. 4, 68–71.

3. Gurnall, *Christian in Complete Armour*, I:278.

4. Ibid.

5. Rod Dreher, *The Benedict Option: A Strategy for Christians in a Post-Christian Nation* (New York: Sentinel, 2017).

6. Gurnall, *Christian in Complete Armour,* I:119, my emphasis.

7. Gurnall, *Christian in Complete Armour,* I:114.

8. Martin Lloyd-Jones, *The Christian Warfare* (Grand Rapids: Baker Books, 1976) and *The Christian Soldier* (Grand Rapids: Baker Books, 1977).

9. J. C. Ryle, *Expository Thoughts on the Gospels,* Vol. Four: John 10:10–End (1874; Grand Rapids: Zondervan Publishing House, 1951), 353.

10. Isaac Watts, "Am I a Soldier of the Cross," *Trinity Hymnal,* #573, 2nd stanza.

11. Lloyd-Jones, "Who Does the Fighting," in *The Christian Soldier*, 40–53.

12. Charles Wesley, "Soldiers of Christ, Arise," *Trinity Hymnal,* #575, stanzas 1, 2.

13. Ibid., stanza 3.

14. Sabing Baring-Gould, "Onward Christian Soldiers," in *Trinity Hymnal*, #572, stanzas 1–3.

Chapter 10. Concluding Considerations

1. Gurnall, *Christian in Complete Armour,* I:12.

2. Stephen Charnock, *Discourses Upon the Existence and Attributes of God,* Volumes I and II (1682; Grand Rapids: Baker Book House, 1979), II:466 (my emphasis); also available in *The Works of Stephen Charnock*, Volumes I and II (Edinburgh: The Banner of Truth Trust, 2010).

3. Charnock, *Existence and Attributes*, II:390.

4. Gurnall, *Christian in Complete Armour*, II:14.

5. Charnock, *Existence and Attributes,* II:468–69.

6. Henry F. Schaefer III, *Science and Christianity: Conflict or Coherence?* (Watkinsville, GA: The Apollos Trust, 2003).

7. See B. B. Warfield, "It says: Scripture Says: God Says," in *The Inspiration and Authority of the Bible* (1929; Philadelphia: Presbyterian and Reformed Publishing; 1948), 245–348.

8. Charnock, *Existence and Attributes,* II:467.

9. Ibid., II:468.

10. J. I. Packer, *Knowing God* (Downers Grove, IL: InterVarsity Press, 1973), 22.